The *Wedding* Guide *for the* Grownup Bride

The Wedding Guide for the Grownup Bride

Shelley Christiansen

BERKLEY BOOKS, NEW YORK

This book is an original publication of The Berkley Publishing Group.

THE WEDDING GUIDE FOR THE GROWNUP BRIDE

A Berkley Book / published by arrangement with
the author

PRINTING HISTORY
Berkley trade paperback edition / May 2000

The Penguin Putnam Inc. World Wide Web site address is
http://www.penguinputnam.com

ISBN: 0-425-17436-0

BERKLEY®
Berkley Books are published by The Berkley Publishing Group,
a division of Penguin Putnam Inc., 375 Hudson Street,
New York, New York 10014.
BERKLEY and the "B" design
are trademarks belonging to Penguin Putnam Inc.

PRINTED IN THE UNITED STATES OF AMERICA

10 9 8 7 6 5 4 3 2 1

In remembrance of my other guys,

Acknowledgments

Blossoms from the bouquet to the consultants, couturiers, gift registrars, stationers, and other wedding warriors who unloaded lessons learned; wise *and warm* attorney Joan Wilbon; Jessica Faust, who pounced on the idea; Lisa Considine, who nudged it gently to fruition; Marie Brown, who led the child through the wilderness; dear friends whose personal episodes and sentiments have wound up in print; Mom, my supreme source and buddy; and Trond, *min kjaereste*, for infinitely more than I can explain.

Contents

PART THREE
*With This Ring, I Thee Blend into
the Rest of My Life Somehow*

~

Why This Book

After my friend Cheryl gave birth years ago, she was nearly compelled to call a press conference. "I feel like no one's ever done this before!" she exclaimed.

Having a human emerge from one's loins is probably more profound than starting a marriage, but the analogy works: There's no comparable, prior experience that can prepare anyone for either event.

Never mind that billions of women have wed before us. First-timers blaze this wilderness alone, and it's mysterious. That holds true for teenagers, senior citizens and all of us in between. It holds true in Kuwait as well as Kansas. It held true in the Middle Ages, and it holds true now.

So why do we mid-lifers need our own special book?

A fair question. It's hardly extraordinary anymore for brides to be in mid-life. But we're ambiguous. New but not fresh. This became clear to me on my first trip to a bridal salon. My fellow customers were an ingenue and her mother:

"We've been here three hours. You've tried on 15 gowns. Make a decision."

"Umm . . . let's check out the other shop down the street."

I was suddenly sandwich filling, squished between two peers. Like one peer, I aimed to act with grownup efficiency. Hey, let's tick off another item on the "to do" list and move on. Like the other peer, I wanted my first and, of course, only Big Day the way I wanted it, no matter what it took.

Mid-life brides are a breed slightly apart. Sure, like younger brides, we feel exhilarated, dreamy, nervous and, well, young. But not entirely young: We're wiser but jaded. We're more decisive but perhaps more stubborn. We're more self-reliant, more skilled in life management. But we're poorer in time and energy. We've got more emotional and physical baggage. We've heard many a marital war story from our peers, and maybe we've starred in one ourselves. We're pulled in more directions—by demanding jobs, aging parents, work, maybe teenagers, maybe health problems, maybe all of the above.

Can we begin new lives when we aren't so new ourselves? Adapting—to new languages, gearshifts, or lifestyles—just seems easier when we're young.

Some "mid-lifers" are as young as, say, 28, if they've been tackling the world on their own with full intensity for a few years. Most of us mid-lifers are over 40. And I suspect that marriage is "simpler," if not always better, for women who've come of age at any time *but* the '60's.

The baby boom yielded a historically odd breed of coddled, middle-class kids with few worries and abundant free time, and we spent much of it bending society's rules. Sex out of wedlock was so acceptable, it was practically required. What's more, it was "free," with the availability of birth control and the legalization of abortion. AIDS wasn't even a notion.

College education was more widely available than ever, and it trained us to think, not just obey. Hence, every institution and authority came open to question. We decried government. We protested war. We confronted religious doctrine. Those of us who were "Negro" redefined ourselves "black" and defied second-class citizenship.

Young women, too, began to recognize and defy second-class citizenship. Whatever the guys could do, we could and should do, too. We could be doctors or auto mechanics. We could go braless. We could ask men out on dates. We could even date around. Marriage and motherhood were fully optional. *How* to get married and be married was up to our judgment, too. Many a young wedding couple stood barefoot and tie-dyed at a garden altar. Even the traditional white-dress-and-chapel affair often included original vows or some other small rebellion. "Ave Maria" often stepped aside for "We've Only Just Begun."

Our heads may have been at Woodstock. Nonetheless, our umbilical cords were plugged into Betty Crocker, and she was no pushover. In our formative years, our destinies as brides, housewives and mothers had been lovingly charted by Mom, Dad, Cinderella, *Good Housekeeping*, home economics teachers, baby dolls and television mothers *à la* Harriet Nelson. Consciously or not, willfully or not, we bring this legacy to the altar, too.

I once asked my mother what she got out of being married. Answer: "Security . . . companionship . . . family . . . oh, and love!"

Now add to this recipe of mid-life and the Age of Aquarius a whole lot of years of independent living. Some mid-life brides may be on the rebound from recent divorce, gravitating toward a familiar comfort zone of foot warming, dinner chat and all. Others have been involved with their husbands-to-be for a seeming eternity. But many of us have been flying solo for a long time. Decades, even. Our most familiar zone is a solitary and private one with a single captain. Sounds like a bad omen for effective coupling.

After all, life is good. We make a living. We have friends and pastimes. We have homes, and they're decorated just the way we want them. We come and go as we please. We spend, save and invest as we want. We may eat corn flakes for dinner. We can sleep spread-eagled, diagonally across the whole bed. Our floors are littered with house slippers and dog toys. Or some of us are neat to the max, and there's no one leaving their socks on the floor.

Are we lonely? At times. But most of the time, our mood is better described as peaceful. "Without being in despair, I was finally liking my solitude." So said Barbra Streisand to *People* magazine, reflecting on her state of mind after some 25 years of being single—just prior to meeting second husband James Brolin.

At the extreme, a few of us mid-lifers are first-timers. And I do mean few: Some researchers or wise-asses—I'm not sure which—have observed that a woman past 40 is more likely to get struck by lightning or killed by a terrorist than to marry for the first time. I don't doubt it.

"I never could have predicted that at the somewhat geriatric age of 42, I would meet the man I finally would want to marry," said television journalist Diane Sawyer to an interviewer. "Now what are the odds on that?" A snowball's chance in Hades.

"I never even came close to considering marriage before John," said a woman named Jeanne. "Love, for sure. Living together, too. But not marriage. It wasn't one of my goals."

Why are we waiting so late to marry? Most of us believe we're marrying right on time. Jeanne's young stepdaughter is leaving her husband of two years. "When I think about myself and my girlfriends," Jeanne reflects, "almost all of us got married in our thirties or forties. None of us is divorced and, to my knowledge, all of us have strong marriages."

In 1999, marriage researchers at Rutgers University considered two interesting pieces of data: America's median age of marriage has gradually risen. Simultaneously, the divorce rate has leveled off. The researchers suspect a strong link between aging and stable marriages.

Indeed, as we consider the very young bride, we must beware a tendency to be smug. We may feel smarter than she is about marriage. We figure if we had little sense at that age, surely she has little sense, too. Wisdom may grow with age and experience, but it's hardly guaranteed. There's many a desperate, cunning or confused mid-life woman out there. On the flip side, some young brides are indeed clear-thinking and self-knowing. Their biggest handicap may be that they don't know the selves they or their grooms will be 20 years down the road. They're still in formation. Fortunate couples form compatibly.

Woe to the narrow-minded observer who thinks mid-life first-timers are simply old maids who've been of no interest to Cupid! Cupid's arrows have a hard time piercing targets in perpetual motion. Or perpetual armor.

Before taking the plunge, I lived 46 years as a supreme bachelorette. Childhood friends would ask, "Don't you hate being an only child?"

Odd question; I had no frame of reference. And what was to hate? I didn't have to put my head down sideways on the table to make sure my siblings and I had level shares of Kool Aid. I watched *my* favorite cartoons. Listened to *my* favorite records. Slept in *my* bed and bedroom. I got all the Christmas presents, too, but that was hardly important. What I valued most about only-childhood was peace. I never had to negotiate or fight. I was gladly generous with friends and even strangers. But *sharing*? That was a tougher nut.

"Shelley's sooo independent," I once overheard a camp counselor say in a complimentary tone.

"Shelley's always been very independent," I've often heard my mother say in a clinical manner to explain some odd behavior of mine.

"You're very independent," a boss once told me during an exit interview. "That's not necessarily a bad quality, but it doesn't work here."

Come to think of it, despite six siblings and a traditional marriage that began at age 24, my mother was quite the role model for independence herself. She deferred major decisions to my father, but when it came to everyday management—fixing things, hauling stuff, scolding me—she just took care of it. No image of her has ever been more impressive to me than the sight of her pulling the guts out of the back of the television cabinet. Surrounded by tubes, tools and wires, she nearly always vanquished "snow" or horizontal roll. Depression families didn't rear princesses.

Aunt Bern was yet another kind of model—single, self-sufficient, and bouncy of gait. The Bern picture is hardly complete without her green-trimmed white suitcase. Summer vacations from classroom teaching took her to Europe, Hawaii and Mexico. Christmas always brought her to us, often with gifts from afar. Proper to the max, Bern may well have considered marriage socially preferable to being single. And beneath the cheerful humming, for all I know, she may have sorely missed the companionship of a man. Or not: Maybe she privately had one. But the Aunt Bern I grew up knowing was autonomous and terrific at it.

Like most girls, I loved weddings. The big white dress, the flowers, the music, the kiss, the cake. Yet whenever I heard *till death do you part* or *as long as you both may live,* I couldn't help but hear the resounding slam of a prison gate. Time to catch the bouquet? I'll pass.

Early in my dating career, Mark served to reaffirm my solitary bent. For nearly three years, *we* struggled to find himself. Our relationship revolved around *his* life problems until, one day, *I* had a problem: Suddenly laid off from my job, I was hurt and scared. He basically shrugged. Love had worn me out. For a loooong time thereafter, the men I sporadically dated were sweet and entertaining but unavailable or just plain ill-suited for marriage. Just like me. I eventually stumbled upon a greeting card with a picture of a nude female biker, leaning into the wind, hair flying. She looked as unbought and unbossed as Shirley Chisholm, as brazen as Madonna. I bought the card and framed it.

Then Aunt Bern stunned the whole family by marrying for the first time at age 70. Hmmmm. Starting the second "career" after retiring from the first. Now there was a compelling approach. Maybe it could work for me. Meantime, being footloose was a badge of honor, and I wore it well. *You do your thing, and I'll do mine.*

As I approached age 40, my "thing" slowed down considerably. I still enjoyed extracurricular contact with the world, but after a full day, my idea of "happy hour" was usually my sofa. Maybe slow motion was the reason I noticed Future Husband when he crossed my path. To my delight and astonishment, I was ready, and I knew it.

Ready for marriage, that is. But for a wedding? The dawn of a new life phase certainly warrants a moment of ceremony. To us mid-life brides, however, the ceremony is just that—a moment. It's a fleeting ritual at the threshhold of the real deal. The ultimate point is to *be* married, not *get* married.

Still, the wedding comes first, chronologically. So how do we do it? And we mean how do we do it in a grown-up fashion? Furthermore, how do we find time to do it? We've got other things to take care of in our lives.

And, yes, what about those other things? What about our families? Careers? Finances? Any lingering need for space? How do we prepare to blend marriage with all *that*?

For mid-lifers of all ages, here are some observations and ideas from the consummate inexperienced, independent bride.

PART ONE

Forget the Wedding. Prepare for Marriage.

The Roar of the Diamond: Engagement

Dinner at the restaurant where we had our first date. Wine and candlelight. After the remnants of trout are whisked away, Future Husband takes my hand affectionately. But what's this hard nugget in the midst of our grasp? Oh, shoot!

Marriage is one thing, but being *engaged*? Do we need this?

Besides, I thought of us as being engaged already. Like many couples, we'd been contemplating marriage for a while, working our way from innuendo to straight talk. *He'd* been babbling about lifelong togetherness since our third date. This flame's going to fizzle fast, I worried. I also worried it wouldn't.

Valentine's Day: He gave me some lovely citrine earrings, mumbling something akin to an apology. "I really wanted to get you something more special, but the time's not right yet. I hope you understand." Translation: My sons are still reeling from my divorce. It's too soon to deliver the next blow.

Hey, I was just happy to be someone's Valentine for two years straight, after more than a decade of feeling alienated by the whole holiday. Although matrimonial thoughts were mutual by then, I had no deadline in mind. I was supremely satisfied with the status quo—love, companionship, a fuzzy beard against my cheek. If we could only live closer and stop commuting, life would be perfect.

What's more, Future Husband had given me a tourmaline ring upon returning from a business trip a year earlier. No explanation attached, other than some mumbling about the good deals to be had on gems in South America. The pretty green and benign-looking stone was my special token. A grownup version of the friendship rings proudly worn by college girls when they were "sort of engaged to be engaged." Unlike most college girls, I kept its significance private.

So one day, I figured, we'd quietly, seamlessly make the transition into matrimony. But now he's slipping me a solitaire and Popping the Question! He's making it official, and it's a little scary. Not even as a teenager had I ever rehearsed this scene. "Yes," she squeaked. (It was an out-of-body thing.) She didn't even want dessert.

But this *ring*! Instantly, it conjured up ghosts of my youth—the ones who looked down upon diamond engagement rings as bourgeois. Socially dictated. Predictable. Devoid of individual expression. Moreover, in the days of apartheid, diamonds had been politically incorrect in many eyes, mine included. DeBeers and the like had grown fat off the land and labor of oppressed South Africans. And like the death of Jim Crow, the death of apartheid is a slow work in progress.

Not without guilt, I loved the ring. So round, perfect, and "simple," just like love. Shopping for the ring *with* Future Husband would have been more practical; mid-life women like that. Yet surprise presentations are more romantic; mid-lifers like that, too. Here again, we're on that fence between liberation and old-fashioned sentiment.

According to one jeweler, the typical man in mid-life has the wisdom *not* to buy a ring before having a firm indication that his intended wants to marry him. Many a younger customer returns to the store with his tail between his legs.

For the 72 hours the ring was out of my grasp for resizing, I imagined how it must feel to be a new mother whose baby's been whisked from her arms to the hospital nursery.

Engagement was an odd place. Being married is very grownup. Even having a "boy" friend is ageless. But being a *fee-ahn-say* seemed a bit formal and *jeune fille*. And now I couldn't even be subtle about it, because I had a screaming solitaire on my hand—a weathered, middle-aged hand.

Could I wear gloves to work the next day? I recalled with some terror all the clamor that erupted every time a 20-something coworker announced she was engaged or pregnant. But after half a morning of holding my hand behind my back, under my arm, in my pocket, under my desk, I gave up. The fastest way to get this over with was to call my secretary—town crier of the department—into my office. I showed her the ring, she screamed, ran out, and faster than E-mail, I was surrounded by eight clucking young women.

"Congratulations!! Oops, we're supposed to congratulate *him*, not you."

News to me. Anyway, I found I rather enjoyed their bubbly good wishes, but that wasn't the end of it. They wanted details: Is it the bearded guy who comes around sometimes? How, when and where did you meet? How, when and where did he propose? Were you surprised or did you see it coming? When's the wedding? Where's the wedding? Big or small? Geez, I don't know! I gently threw everyone out.

Our closest personal friends—women our age—are hardly more grownup about this kind of news. No matter how gray-haired or crow's-footed, some revert to adolescence. One friend screamed like a steam whistle and scared the daylights out of me. Another exploded into tears. I wasn't this moved when *I* got the news. When she recovered, she tearfully confessed she'd been dreaming of marriage for me for 20 years. I'd been dreaming for 18 months, maybe.

Let's be patient with the uproar. Our peers include:

- Longtime wives

- Divorced longtime wives

- Long-divorced short-term wives

- Never-marrieds with long-term boyfriends

- Never-marrieds on the loose.

Statistically speaking, our peers in age are different from us. They married at earlier ages in an earlier era. Or they've never married at all. Yet what do we all have in common? We're all past our prime years of meeting and dating men. No more streams of prospects, however thin those streams in the first place. In our thirties, we found this creeping realization frightful. By age 40, we were merely resigned. And thank goodness, there are no more endless, adolescent phone calls among us, scrutinizing late developments and next steps. *Do you think I should call him?* There's still the occasional date or affair. Kudos to the unsung men who are more attracted to us than to Gidget. But First Date no. 713 hardly triggers a conference call. Without group consensus, we know—or think we know—by the second drink or bite of lunch if we need to bother seeing 713 again.

Now, for the first time in years, our friends have a rock-solid romance and impending wedding to get excited about. It's a vicarious experience. It makes everyone feel a little giddy.

The friends I'm talking about here are the ones we see and talk to regularly. They've been witnessing, perhaps with awe, our gradual transformation from solo act into lovebird. Our engagement may surprise them, but they're not puzzled by it. A few of my friends had seen it coming from way down the road, and they would say as much. I would just smile and change the subject.

Over the years, however, we've amassed a wider collection of friends and acquaintances who've grown distant from us through time, space or lifestyle. There's the college roommate we haven't seen in 20 years. There's the running buddy we partied with in that other city we used to live in. There's the ex-boyfriend or ex-spouse we occasionally call. In the minds of these people, our roles are frozen in time—maybe as career maniacs, bookish recluses, silly young things, or that woman biker on the greeting card. Anything but an eligible wife. When they hear we're getting married, they may look at the news askance. Can't blame them.

Yet even the most bubbly of our peers are a jaded, cynical lot. Among us, we've known or witnessed hundreds of aggregate woman-years of disappointments in love: opportunities blown, expectations dashed, emptiness, insensitivity, control, deception, extreme compromise, divorce, near-divorce, maybe even abuse. We know "forever" isn't guaranteed. Even the most satisfied in love have known headaches in paradise.

"Girl, it ain't been easy," a happily married friend tells me—repeatedly.

But like a mushroom I once saw rising through fresh asphalt, hope springs eternal. The Society of the Unattached cheers us out of the ranks. The Sisterhood of Wives welcomes us into the fold. It feels oddly conspiratorial.

There may be exceptions. Least inspired to turn cartwheels are the friends with the freshest of wounds. My marriage plans coincided with the divorce plans of my girlfriend of longest standing. Her first divorce, some 20 years ago, had seemed easier. "I'm me again!" she proclaimed, diving headfirst into young single life again. Ending the second, longer marriage was another story, featuring a nonconsenting partner, a custody dispute, financial issues and the general weariness of mid-life. To these details, add feelings of failing twice. "Everyone's allowed *one* mistake," lamented my friend. "But two. . . ."

From the opposite coast, I hoped she could sense my depth of concern for her circumstances, even as I embarked on my own fairy tale. To her, perhaps I seemed like Cinderella—an innocent unprepared for mice and pumpkins down the road. But we were both on the same page, in a way. We'd both arrived at the mountaintop—life's midpoint—seen the promised land and found it wanting. We had both made bold adjustments in the interest of happily-ever-after.

One on one, engagement doesn't feel much different from pre-engagement. Nor does it seem much different from engagements of the young. I was once in the presence of a 60-something corporate executive and his 50-something fiancée at a romantic resort a week before their wedding. They held hands, grinned and looked darn goofy. But they were the happiest-looking couple I'd ever seen, and I couldn't help but feel their spirit. Aunt Bern and her husband were also funny-looking hand-holders in love. Future Husband and I held hands, too—still do. I occasionally wondered if we looked silly to others, without caring one bit. Only our hand-holding conversations changed somewhat, after engagement, to include talk of marriage and wedding plans amid the usual discourse between two lovers and friends.

At work, the lights in the elevator make the solitaire dance if I hold my hand just so. . . .

On Engagement . . . Consider This

• **How should you break the news that you're getting married?** If you're bashful about it, get it over with quickly. You can tell the friend, the relative and the coworker who can be counted on to tell the many. E-mail is even more efficient, though some still find it impersonal.

• **Be prepared to be outed.** It's fine and even fun to keep your engagement a secret, but you're a rare woman indeed if you don't confide the biggest impending moment of your life to at least one person. At that point, the secret is out of your control.

• **Don't let reactions take you by surprise.** When the news gets out, intentionally or otherwise, be prepared to handle shock, giddy commotion and lots of questions. Be as forthcoming or reserved as you want to be. If you choose to be reserved, do it with humor or at least an impish smile. Then change the subject.

• **And try not to take offense.** To the mid-lifer, some friends may wisecrack: "Getting married??? You??!!" Some friends may be truly worried for you. But look at your independent self of, say, ten years ago, and you'll realize the news is kind of amazing to you, too. Share a laugh with your mystified friends—and let them know you've evolved. Don't worry if they doubt it.

• **Be tactfully honest about the ring thing.** It's yet another lifelong commitment. If you don't want a ring, say so. If you'd prefer something other than a diamond, say so. If you're presented with a ring that's simply not your taste, say so and ask if you might pick something else—together.

• **Ring advice to the guys:** Gauge Future Wife's personality. Would she prefer an advance discussion about rings? Or would she be more delighted with the element of thoughtful, creative and romantic surprise—even if she decides to return or exchange your selection?

• **More ring advice to the guys:** "Of course, women who are a little older prefer a *real* diamond—at least a carat or carat and a half," said a jeweler to my husband. Rightfully offended, he departed the store. Frankly, however, a dainty stone is better displayed on a younger hand—or displayed sentimentally on an older hand that's been wearing it since youth. If you need or want to preserve capital, invest in a full-carat birthstone, for example, rather than a quarter-carat diamond solitaire. Or increase the down payment on the new house.

• **If saying *fee-ahn-say* feels juvenile or bourgeois, try something else.** Unfortunately, little else works: *This is my friend Steve.* Your gay buddy next door? *This is my husband-to-be Steve.* Now your lips are in a knot. *This is Steve.* Some guy you met five minutes ago? *This is Steve. We're getting married.* Who asked about your personal agenda? Let's face it: *This is my fiancé Steve* is simple, dignified and to the point. With time and practice, it sounds less peculiar.

• **Be considerate of love's wounded warriors.** Make time and space to be there for them even as you revel in your own heady times.

• **Last but not least, this is the time to plan your marriage.** Where are you going to live? How are you going to comanage finances? More about all this to come . . .

~

Who Is This Dude, Anyway?: Juggling Other Loved Ones

FAMILY

Least effusive about my engagement news was my mother.

"Do you have doubts about him?" I asked.

"No, I have doubts about *you*."

Our parents have been anticipating our wedding days since we were born. Some of us have endured years of hints, sighs, whines, nosy questions and maybe even matchmaking. I was mostly spared. My father staged one awkward matchmaking effort that embarrassed all three of us.

Only once did the subject of marriage come up in conversation. On a long car trip when I was in my thirties, my mother hoped aloud that one day I'd settle into a good marriage. Maybe she was at a stage in life when one looks mortality in the eye and needs to feel everything's in "place."

So ten years later, here I am delivering the Big News on the phone, and she's responding with mere platitudes—not like a mother at all. A little air seeps from my balloon, but I get it. There's no telling exactly when, but at some point over the years my mother probably became reconciled to the fact that I was a solitary soul who was meant to be single and that was okay. With some regret, I suppose, she'd accepted me for who I was. And now I was telling her I was about to try to be someone else. She worried if I was doing the right thing—for me, not for her, God or country. You gotta love a mother for that.

The chronology seems to work like this:

WOMAN OF 16: *"I'm getting married."*
Family tries to lock her in the house.

WOMAN OF 26: *"I'm getting married."*
Family hugs and weeps for joy.

WOMAN OF 36: *"I'm getting married."*
Family must be peeled from the ceiling.

WOMAN OF 46-PLUS: *"I'm getting married."*
Family: ???

Case in point: Some months before she tied the knot, 70-year-old Aunt Bern mused vaguely to a few siblings that she was thinking about it. "Oh?" was the basic response. Old-fashioned Bern, unable to get parental approval from the grave, probably wanted the next best thing: blessings from her brothers and sisters. I think she mainly got puzzlement.

Our generation wants blessings, in a way, too. Marriage isn't personal. It isn't private. It isn't merely about two people, as we may have felt in the '60's. Marriage is about the community. It's about a flock of beaming coworkers in our offices. It's a brick in the foundation of civilization. And now we realize that's kind of nice! Beseeching *approval* is the only anachronistic part. If our suitors went into the parlor to ask our fathers for our hands in marriage, our fathers would laugh out loud. Still, the embrace of well-wishers feels warm and good.

Bonus for parents: Our husband-to-be will probably be more agreeable to them than some of the characters we brought home in our youth. He may be disconcertingly as gray or soft-bellied as they are, but he'll likely have a bank account, a level head and shoes.

If you have children, their reactions to your marriage plans could depend on several factors, such as their ages, their relationships with their fathers, their opinions of the new guy and how badly they think you need somebody. Annette brought to her marriage a young, adopted daughter who seems to regard Bob's entry into the picture as Christmas in August. *First I get a Mom; now I get a Pop, too.*

THE OTHER FAMILY

As statistics have it, mid-life newlywed couples include at least one divorced party—the husband, in my case. And if the first marriage was long and the divorce isn't old, the previous wife retains substantial equity as Dad's wife, son's wife, brother's wife, coworker's wife, etc. We Janie-come-latelies may be welcomed. We may be merely tolerated. Or we may take it on the chin. Whatever the case, no one will likely accuse us of being "some young chippie" exploiting his mid-life crisis.

I was on the brink of becoming a stepparent—an awkward role faced by millions before me. I yearned to be Dad's Sort-of-Cool Wife. I feared I'd just be Some Strange Woman with whom father would have to be shared from now on. Younger fathers than Future Husband might have had small, impressionable children for their fiancées to meet. But I would be meeting a college student and a teenager; I could expect both to have X-ray vision. I struggled with what to wear. I rehearsed first lines. I sweated the final moments—in one case, simply awaiting a knock on the door. Why did I have on stretch pants? In the other case, I waited for a head of blond curls to emerge from International Arrivals at Kennedy Airport.

"You're holding my shoulder a little too tight," I said to Future Husband as we scanned a sea of travelers.

"Sorry, I just thought you might need a little extra support."

As usual, reality proved much easier than anticipation. Future Stepson and I were bashful but unpanicked.

I may never know the reality of meeting my parents-in-law. They were still bitter about their son's divorce from his first wife when they learned he planned to take a second. He was pouring salt in the first family's wounds, and I was his accomplice.

Like many of our own parents, my in-laws believe marriage is meant to be forever. For better or for worse, you stick it out. "You're in this for the long haul," my mother admonished me before my own nuptials in a finger-wagging tone. I know. *Till death do you part.* That's one of the hundred reasons marriage gave me the chills up until recently.

My in-laws may have been on the verge of softening when they got the second blow: I was racially "incorrect." Disappointment bloomed into a gaping impasse between son and parents, causing my mother to worry that he'd be talked into calling off the wedding. But that's another plus of marrying in mid-life: Parental pressure *might* work on a 25-year-old but not on a longtime grownup with seasoned confidence in his own judgment. On the downside, longtime grownups and their parents have precious little time in which to achieve reconciliation.

FLUFFY AND FIDO

"I suppose you're going to write something about the cat," grumbled my husband.

Of course.

Many a pet has suffered the burden of a new love distracting its owner and rendering her silly. *Why does she need this Bozo,* wonders Fido or Fluffy, *when she's got me?* We may have had our pets since we were young women in need of something cuddly and reliable between boyfriends. Now we're in mid-life, and our pets are geriatric. Even the snootiest of cats wants more cuddle time now. Older pets take enormous comfort in the status quo.

In our many years together, I think Jackson had considered himself more my mate than my cat. After all, he was the most constant male around. The best reception a male visitor could expect was the evil eye. *Isn't it about time you were leaving?* At the other extreme, one visitor got bitten on the toe at the ultimate inopportune moment.

To my amazement, on Future Husband's second visit, Jackson curled up in his lap. Trying to make a sweet impression? Trying to pin him down? Some time later, I received a dozen roses. Jackson didn't try to eat them!! These behaviors were getting my attention. *This one's a keeper.* . . . .

Future Husband, who was also in the good-impression stage of courtship, demonstrated remarkable cat tolerance. He's a dog person. Dogs, vis-à-vis cats, are better at softening up men, and vice versa. Dogs look *up* to people; men like that. Cats can be spooky; men *don't* like that. Even if natural attraction should fail, an obedient dog will be civil to our guy upon our command. But if the dog's been trained to protect us from intruders all these years, our new man is still guilty until proven otherwise.

Jackson was endured for my sake. I was lucky. Despite best efforts, sometimes we must make painful choices between our man and our pet. If our pet is old, finding a new home for him isn't easy. And he's less likely than our man to make snide remarks when we reach for our reading glasses. Yet we realize our pet's less likely to rub our bad knees in old age.

TOUGH CHOICES

Some loved ones not only love us; they need us, too. Younger brides sometimes bring whining toddlers in tow. Our loved ones in need are more likely to be elderly parents and relatives or perhaps the disabled lady next door. They may rely on us to drive them to the store, to help with the tax returns, to listen. We may have teenagers or college students. Of course, they don't "need" us—except to cook, clean, lend cars and fork over cash.

Now we're getting married, and no matter how happy all these people may be for us, they'll wonder: Will we be too busy for them? Too distracted? Will we move away? We may not be sure of the answers ourselves.

I could not commit to a marriage, let alone announce one, before weighing the consequences for the people to whom I already felt most committed. My father was fully disabled by Parkinson's disease. My mother was his primary supporter, and she wasn't getting younger. Their primary supporter has been me, sort of. Separated by 250 miles and my mother's dogged resistance to help, my "support" was reduced mainly to nagging on the phone. Nonetheless, I hadn't forgotten that they'd devoted their lives to nurturing, spanking, spoiling and believing in me. Future Husband might love me every bit as much, but he didn't have seniority.

I first broached the subject with my mother sometime between the tourmaline and the diamond. So, Mom: I was maybe thinking about pondering the contemplation of weighing the consideration of, uh, getting married. The man in question has a job that could send us back home to Norway or to the ends of the earth, for that matter. In fact, he's already a thousand miles from here. *Whither thou goest* . . . you always said that's a wife's role. But if you're not comfortable with that, I need to know. How would you feel? Really?

She said something predictable, like "You know I'd never come between you and your dreams."

I asked how you *felt.*

"Well, I really can't say. I have to weigh things as they happen."

The world is smaller today, Mom. I'd always be just a phone/plane/fax/E-mail away. . . .

It's darn hard not to rationalize, and it's hard to keep the rationalizing out of the discussion. But try we must.

Mom had a realistic point: It's nearly impossible for some people to situate themselves in abstract scenarios. She was willing to climb aboard my adventure and see where it led. She was game. But I made myself listen to what she *didn't* say, too. If the tendons in her neck had transmitted fear or sorrow, I would have had some fundamental, life-altering compromises to make. I don't know what they might have been. But I'm sure they would have been unsatisfying.

Talking to our loved ones is just the beginning of the issue. We should then do some scenario planning on our own. What if our sister has to have a major operation, and we're living in Taiwan? Will we rush back to look after her kids? What if Mom can't live alone anymore? Does she come live with us? Do we go live with her? Do we find a live-in companion or assisted-living facility?

Have we overlooked something? Probably we've overlooked our future husbands! We're so accustomed to bearing burdens with two shoulders and making decisions with one mind, that these habits are etched in stone. But we're not sole proprietors anymore. We're embarking on a partnership, and it's not a part-time partnership. We share our whole lives, human baggage included. What a relief. What an imposition. What a conundrum.

It's helpful when both parties bring roughly equal outside commitments into the marriage. I support Future Husband's commitment to his sons. If they ever need guy time for themselves, fine! Should they ever want to live with us, fine! He supports my commitment to my parents. If they need to move in with us, fine! If I want to take "time off" to see to their needs, fine! The latter agreement worries me a little. For all his understanding and caring, my husband is still a high-maintenance kind of man. He wants me close.

On Other Loved Ones . . .
Consider This

• *Don't* keep your marriage plans secret from your most significant people. Dependents and others to whom you're emotionally or materially attached deserve to know. And they deserve to know it from you first.

• Get emotional support in the event of family discord. Family amazement may either amuse or disappoint you. But outright anger is distressing. The good news is, we've got at least one loved one squarely on our marriage's side. Share your troubles with your man, and help shoulder any troubles on his side. Don't hesitate to confide in loving friends. They'll come through as surrogate family. Time, calm talk, the endurance of familial love, or respect for the institution of marriage may eventually soothe the unhappy. They may agree to disagree. At the very least, they'll probably grow weary of voicing their complaints against your deaf ears.

• **Listen to any concerns**—expressed or implied, real or imagined—your loved ones may have about their future relationships with you. Plan for the maintenance of those relationships as specifically as possible. Don't promise people that everything will be "the same" if things may in fact change. Do assure people that your love, interest, and commitment to them are undiminished.

• **Seek Future Husband's endorsement of commitments to others.** Assure him that he'll get the same from you. Don't make assumptions. *Of course he understands I have to look after Aunt Bessie.* Tell him, and spell out what "looking after" means.

• **Introduce the real you to your in-laws.** You're mature enough to know not to impersonate Alexis Carrington, Mary Poppins, Ginger Spice or anyone else who isn't the woman they'll know for a lifetime. Moreover, you know the real you is just fine, thank you. Of course, for first impression's sake, you'll want to put forward the *best* of the real you. Try not to obsess over what to wear or cook. Focus instead on transmitting that you're simply joining Future Husband's fan club, not stealing him from it.

~

Baby?: The Motherhood Question

"Are you married?" a six-year-old asked me.

"No."

"Do you have any children?" asked her friend.

"No."

"How come? Don't you want any? Do you think you'll have some soon?"

I was a 21-year-old college intern working in an urban first-grade classroom, facing an inquisition by a group of children perplexed by an "aging," childless woman. Now fast-forward a quarter-century. As these former first-graders probably drop their own first-graders at school, I sit in my office fielding an inquiry from the bridal welcome wagon: "Are you going to have any children?"

The question catches me off guard now as much as it did then. Yet I would hear this more than once, after my marriage plans went public. Questions, suggestions and near-assumptions about me and motherhood surprised me routinely. *Next, we'll be giving you a baby shower. Tee hee.* What was wrong with these people? If they thought I was a younger woman, I'm flattered. More likely, they figured I might make a last-ditch effort at childbirth in my sunset years of ovulation. In case they suspected I was already making "progress," I wore fitted clothing and tried to suck in my tummy at all times.

No bride or groom of any age can afford to make assumptions about her or his partner's family goals. At our age, fortunately, most of us are at least clear about our *own* goals. Either we want a child by any means necessary, or No way, José.

In the rose-colored days of early romance—sometime after the "growing old together" thing—Future Husband wondered aloud what our children might look like. I giggled and shuddered at the same time. Months later, with his feet on the ground, he admitted he had no ambition to begin fatherhood anew. Snotty noses, puberty, Spaghetti-Os on the floor . . . been there, done that. He loves his sons more than he loves anyone. He delights in their forays into young adulthood. He misses them deeply when they're not around. But nowadays, collecting antique silver is a more appealing pastime for him than molding a human being from scratch.

Timidly, he asked if that was okay with me. It absolutely was, though hearing the question aloud forced me for the first time to address the issue head-on. Like marriage, motherhood was never one of my goals; nor was it a must-avoid. Both these concepts had sat on my back burner on "warm." As I approached age 40, fears of birth defects pretty much cooled my motherhood burner for good. *Ma'am, your amniocentesis results are a little troubling. . . .*

Still, many women our age want desperately to become mothers. The need is central to their sense of identity. For some, no medical procedure or expense is too extreme. Thanks to modern health care and modern attitudes, it's no longer shocking to see a woman with graying hair and a big belly—and a smile. Or they choose adoption, sometimes going literally to the ends of the earth to make it happen. Lately, there's been an adopted-baby boom among a host of *single* baby boomers I know. Mid-life mothers hope to be alive and standing for graduations, weddings and the birth of the next generation. More power to them.

Prevailing wisdom has it that newlyweds should be a twosome for a while before becoming a threesome. Unfortunately, mid-life couples don't feel they have such a luxury, and they're probably right. Their marriages often start off under pressure to conceive.

Sometimes, of course, the most fervent motherhood effort fails, and dreams die. I strongly sympathize, but I hardly empathize. Fortunately, it's socially acceptable today to be an "unnatural" woman in this respect. It remains miraculous to me that every day, billions of ordinary people all over the world rear children—bathing, dressing, feeding, holding them—without accidentally killing or maiming the delicate mortals. On a rare baby-sitting job, I failed at fastening a diaper—an idiotproof *disposable* diaper. Yet mothers and fathers successfully teach their children values, manners, arithmetic, how to hold a fork or hammer and why the pet goldfish had to die. People achieve all this and more without the natural instincts of an orangutan or even a toll-free technical support number.

I've barely had role models for motherhood. I've had no brothers, sisters, nieces, or nephews. Cousins have been born and raised in other places. Few of my close friends have had children. My mother was of course a mother—and happy to be one, more often than not. But it's hardly possible to be a third-party observer of motherhood when one is the second party.

Motherhood also seems the ultimate loss of freedom. There's nowhere you can go, nothing you can do without first answering the question *What about the baby?* A visit to Washington by my uncle's ten-year-old goddaughter served only to back up my theory. The end of the week left me gratified, entertained and exhausted to the bone. Fine. The disconcerting part was, I didn't have a single moment all week to be just me.

"If you have a baby, you won't *be* the baby anymore," said the mother of a spoiled Goldie Hawn character contemplating motherhood in the movie *Overboard*. That, too, struck a chord. For me, maybe a baby was as threatening as younger brothers and sisters were when I was a child. Given a fresh, cute newcomer, maybe no one would love me anymore.

On the other hand: I love children. I've delighted in my first-graders, my uncle's goddaughter, and my teenage cat-and-plant sitter in the apartment down the hall. I've eagerly gotten out of bed on Saturday mornings in the dead of winter to coach a bunch of bright, eager high school journalism students. I continuously threaten two beloved, long-distance godchildren with Big Fat Sloppy Wet Kisses and take enormous pride in my status as vice-parent. Family reunions delight me mainly for the merry bands of second and third cousins who are the life of the party. I love mature conversations with collegians and 20-somethings, who are—yikes!—just the age my own children would be today, if I'd had some.

At Christmas, it's pitiful to find that even in my forties, I've been the closest manifestation of a kid on the home front. I can't help but feel responsible. My parents would be the world's best grandparents, and I've never come through.

During the Gulf War, one CNN reporter volunteered to stay on the scene while his colleagues retreated to safety. Why? They had spouses and children; he didn't. The reporter's noble gesture sent a chill through my body. I, too, was dispensable. Posterity wasn't dependent upon me. Melodramatic as it may sound, I was unnecessary. Funny, how diminishing freedom can sometimes be.

One of these days, I may have grandchildren! (Note to stepsons: Don't rush it.) They won't inherit the fluorescent Moore grin, but I'll spoil, spank, teach, and love them as if they shared my blood. Then I'll send them home! If they survive, that is. At least I now know the secret to successful diapering.

On Motherhood . . .
Consider This

• **Settle the parenthood issue.** If you two haven't already discussed your respective goals, do it now. Don't assume what your partner has in mind. Don't underestimate your own desires. Compromise is always possible, but this is one of the toughest compromise nuts there is. If the decision is a deal breaker, better to break the partnership before it's signed and sealed.

• **Hurry up!** Younger newlyweds, if they're wise, will take time to settle into living as two before adding a whining dependent to the mix. Unfortunately, mid-lifers don't have much time on their side. If parenthood is in the plan, get going sooner rather than later. The pulpit apparently agrees: When my friend Gail and her fiancé met with their pastor for premarital counseling, he advised there would be nothing wrong with getting started *before* the wedding. Try not to panic over the urgency of getting pregnant.

• **Don't worry about anyone's concern about your age besides your doctor's.** But yes, do listen to the doctor. Also consult other older mothers; hear the voices of experience. If you don't know any, check the Internet for a relevant chat room.

• **Consider adoption.** Perhaps you're unable to conceive. Maybe you wish to steer clear of the age-related risks of pregnancy. Maybe you feel it's more sensible in mid-life to start with a "middle-aged" child—a fifth-grader, for example, rather than an infant. Or maybe you'd like to combine parenthood with an act of goodwill.

• **Don't worry about anyone else if you *don't* want children.** Some friend or family member may surprise you with the expectation that you should have a child. That person is either old-fashioned or selfish. Ignore.

• **Be a "part-time" parent.** If you want to be around children just *some* of the time, volunteer at a day-care center, hospital, or recreation facility. Find a mentoring opportunity at a school or community organization. Or take in the nephews while your sister's on vacation.

Don't Fax the Florist: Reconciling Job and Marriage

Colleagues will ask, "How are the wedding plans going?"

Here's what we say: "I'm waiting for someone to tell *me*."
Then: "How's the MacNamara proposal coming along?"

Even if our plans are fully under control, we dread that anyone on the job should think our marriages are more on our mind than our work. For we are the Consummate Career Women!

Walk into the office of a man: As he winds up a phone call, you can get a fix on his persona with one sweeping glance. You'll know, for example, that he has a wife and some daughters—"some," because you're looking at photos of either four individual girls or two girls twice, at different ages. You'll know one of them is a near-talented artist. He has a golden retriever, and once upon a time, he caught a tremendous bass. He was named Man of the Year by the Rotary Club.

Look around a woman's office: You'll find a sales award and a souvenir paperweight from the opening of the new plant. If you look carefully, you *may* find one small photo of the kids half hidden behind the pencil cup. That'll be the extent of personal information.

Keeping our private lives this private may be overdoing it, but our paranoia isn't without basis. Most of us work in a traditionally male milieu, where stereotypes about the so-called weaker sex remain entrenched. Even men our ages and younger—exposed to the likes of Gloria Steinem, Helen Reddy, Katharine Graham, Oprah Winfrey—often succumb to Neanderthal instincts about women's priorities. Central to many gender stereotypes are issues of family. We've seen women's career fortunes wane as they take time off to care for a chronically ill child or parent. Conversely, we've witnessed admiration for the occasional Mr. Mom.

Now we're getting married, and if we sport a diamond or otherwise leak the news, the boss knows. Employees who are long-time marrieds are stable and known entities. We, on the other hand, are in personal transition, and many bosses—women included—will wonder if the transition translates into diminishing returns for them. It makes little difference that we're probably more grounded in our orientation to work than many younger brides. The boss may still suspect that marriage will render us less focused, less committed, better able to quit, less likely to work overtime, averse to travel, less willing to relocate, less able to handle the demands of a promotion, or even (as we've discussed) more likely to get pregnant.

This much is likely true: A study conducted in the 1980s revealed that, on average, the most successful career people were married men and single women. This is hardly surprising. Even in today's modern marriages, wives still tend to be the support players. Consequently, work and stress are compounded for married, working women—while married, working men are freer to focus on the job. Making matters tougher for us women in mid-life, our main role models for marriage are our mothers, the last full generation of long-suffering, full-time housewives.

A workaholic and 40-something bride I know used to go home around 5 P.M. every day, cook dinner for her husband, then *return* to the office and work several more hours. "If I don't cook, he won't eat," she explained. Give me a break.

Some bosses go beyond wondering about our postmarital job intentions and pry right in. Those bosses tread thin legal ice. We've got every right to reply, "None of your blankety-blank business, (sir)." Still, their doubts about our changing lives may evolve into setbacks. Paranoia notwithstanding, we may get shorter-term, lower-priority, or less "visible" assignments. Younger women may eventually get their careers back on the good foot, given sufficient drive, savvy, luck, and time. For older brides, this is a tougher nut. We're in mid-career and in striking distance of the glass ceiling—the invisible barrier that tends to cap the rise of women and minorities in the workplace.

Glass-ceiling brides fall into two basic categories.

Category One: For some of us, the crystal ball suggests we've still got a step or two up the ladder in our future. We wonder if marriage or any other sidestep, let alone misstep, might turn the crystal cloudy.

"I don't have time to get married," explains a driven, competitive manager after over two years of engagement and one postponed, never rescheduled wedding date. Well, of course not. No full-time worker has time to marry, have a baby, clean, cook, exercise, read a book, take a vacation, and so on—unless he or she *makes* the time. Norma, however, falls into a category of people who are Married to the Job—an affliction that knows every gender and age but seems to be borne disproportionately by mid-life women. God forbid we get off the career track for so much as an instant.

Fortunately, even the happiest of campers in their careers tend to realize by mid-life that work ain't everything. In an interview with the *Detroit News* years ago, television journalist Diane Sawyer marveled at meeting the man she wanted to marry at the "somewhat geriatric" age of 42—and "at the same time that I was doing the work that gave me the most freedom and happiness."

"Timing is everything," says Jeanne, who quit a rewarding middle-management job to marry and follow her husband overseas. "At an earlier stage in my career, I don't know what I would have done, presented with such a life change. The decision was easier than I'd expected." Her staff was more stunned about her marriage plans than her resignation.

Category Two: Others of us feel the ceiling hard against our scalps. We're fed up and burned out. Some of us are inadequately challenged.

After a quarter-century of stress and diminishing returns, we may be ready for a sabbatical.

I used to marvel at married, work-weary female colleagues who'd contemplate taking off, say, a year or two—or maybe forever—to rest, reflect or restore a barn. *Well, la dee dah.* These ideas never, ever occur to us bachelors. And by the way: Pity the weary *man* who'd dare utter such thoughts in mid-career. He'd likely be censured by boss, wife, in-laws and society at large. His peers might silently empathize, but they'd consider him a fool.

Even if we need or want to remain at the salt mines, we realize we also need A Life. Aerobics, baking bread, hiking the Himalayas, tutoring schoolchildren, deciphering Toni Morrison, long talks with good buddies—these are all worthy diversions. For many years, they may sustain us well. But sooner or later, we know they don't fill all the gaps.

When the day is done, and we need a laugh or a hand to hold, wouldn't it be gratifying to find it's *there* for us when we come home? Furthermore, don't we need to tend to someone else's wounds for a change?

Most of all, we need someone to believe in us unconditionally. No worker finds this at work—not even in the best of jobs. A friend who has sickle-cell anemia has this perspective nailed. Every time she lies in the hospital, wondering if she'll come out on two feet, she hasn't a care in the world about the boss's last tantrum over some trifle. She gets all the validation she needs from her husband and other loved ones. Any reassurance that might come from work is simply gravy. My own perspective congealed when a change of supervisor pushed my job security to an all-time low and my mood into a funk. Future Husband responded by giving me a briefcase for my birthday. I wanted to hit him with it, but I wept instead. His esteem overwhelmed me.

Working women in Categories One and Two alike have begun to seek the Real Stuff in Life to Cling To. It may be a refrain of Mom's era, but again, we are Mom's daughters. In our younger days, the fullness of work may have compensated for lack of Real Stuff. At the very least, work distracted us from it. Or rendered us too tired to pursue it. And truly, work was often less tiresome and more gratifying than some of the jerks we dated. But now, as the glass ceiling looms, some of us give the Real Stuff another shot.

Meantime, on the job: We could take the high road, babbling about honeymoon plans and splitting the atom all at once. Wouldn't that prove to the most backward boss or colleague that we can balance work and personal life as handily as any man? Ha! But if we lay the foundation right, perhaps women who begin their careers in the twenty-first century will find a higher level of workplace enlightenment.

They won't host any banquets for me, however. I quit my job shortly after marrying and helped stereotypes prevail. "It's not because I'm the woman," I jokingly insisted when I announced my resignation to my coworkers. This unprovoked protest sounded silly even to me, and it's probably because I had my doubts. The logic certainly worked: I quit to move to my husband's job location. Commuter marriages are painful enough for established unions; for newlyweds, worse.

For reasons of relocation, health or dependent care, growing numbers of workers are negotiating win-win deals for working remotely. We're in a fast-track age of E-mail, Internet, Intranet, cellular phones, beepers, faxes, videoconferencing and maybe other technology toys by the time this book is in print. Even more amazing are the modern employers who've become hip to the expanding work options those toys afford. Jungles, dining tables and even cars have been transformed into viable workplaces in the farthest corners of the planet.

Unfortunately, my boss was having none of it. Granted, some of my work would best be done by someone within collar-grabbing distance of authority.

So why shouldn't Future Husband have quit and moved instead? That would have been fine, all things being equal. But they weren't. His line of work was more location-sensitive than mine. With his profession, not to mention my glass ceiling, he had more long-term growth potential than I did. He made more money, too.

And yes, there was Mom again on the rear tape deck of my brain: *Whither thou goest, I shall go,* she's always said of a wife's duty, quoting the Bible, molding me.

I first suggested quitting my job to Future Husband back when we were still talking "around" marriage. It would be the simplest way to bring us together geographically. I made the suggestion not only because it made sense, but also, I suppose, because it spared Future Husband from having to bring it up. He didn't hesitate to accept the idea. But as quitting time approached, he felt guilty, and said so repeatedly. He was making me sabotage my career, he believed. "You're not *making* me do this," I kept reminding him. I didn't mind that he was aware he was an accessory to the act.

Still, I'd never in life quit a job without having another job to go to, and it was scary. The final paperwork. The final paycheck. The farewell to benefits—to a pension, most notably. Despite all the logic of the decision, I pictured myself in the gutter. Moreover, I hated the idea of entering a marriage as a dependent. I'd carried my own weight all my adult life, and the thought of becoming something of a sponger was uncomfortable.

Some of us relocating brides need or want to get a new job in our new environs. Maybe we don't have a single career contact there. Maybe we hardly know our way around the block. For certain, we have a significant disadvantage over the young in the job market. Finding a job takes us longer. Polishing the résumé and pounding the pavement can feel diminishing at an age when we want to feel we've "arrived." Absorbing the culture of a new work environment has grown less enchanting, too. Isn't this fun? The truth is, mid-life job hunters often wind up in good, and sometimes better, positions. Many downsized mid-lifers have ended up with bigger salaries on the new job *and* a lump-sum payout from the last.

Rather than look for another job after marriage, I wanted to work independently again. I wanted professional satisfaction and freedom, too. That would make my financial contribution to the household a big question mark, starting out, but that was fine with Future Husband. *It's a setup,* I briefly worried. *He wants me to be the Little Woman, barefoot, if not pregnant, in the kitchen. . . .*

He further encouraged me to pursue some out-of-the-box ideas that promised creative, if not financial, fulfillment. For years, I'd toyed with these ideas while regular jobs ate my energy and gave me license to procrastinate. Had I mentioned those ideas out loud? I guess so. And now he was endorsing them. That was the best part of all.

On Reconciling the Job . . .
Consider This

• **You control the info flow.** At work, how much you broadcast your marital plans will likely mirror the extent to which you've broadcast personal information all along. That means your coworkers already have a good feel for how much prying you'll tolerate. Most will respect that. But marriage is bigger-than-average news, so expect to be the focus of some extra interest, at least temporarily. Be patient and pleasant. In other words, lighten up. When you've had enough, smoothly change the subject. People will get the message.

• **You can control activities, too.** If bridal showers, luncheons, or gifts are workplace traditions you'd rather avoid, confide in an individual who'll be sure to pass the word. Alternatively, it's okay to request adjustments to the standard affair. Cake but no gift, for example. Or just the immediate work group, not the whole building. Clearly communicate that you're not unappreciative; it's just a comfort-level thing.

• **Hide that pastel book.** Keep your wedding planning at home, or at least under wraps. Do not leave your wedding planner on your desk. Same goes for honeymoon brochures and fabric samples for your dress. Do not ask the caterer to fax your menu to the departmental fax machine. If you must make wedding-related phone calls from work, keep them short and to a minimum. If coworkers ask about the status of your preparations, be brief in your response or confine the discussion to lunch hour in the cafeteria. Also, use lunch hours for dress fittings or other appointments, rather than disappearing during work hours. If possible, schedule a few vacation days for planning purposes so you can quit whispering on the phone and looking over your shoulder.

• **Mutually figure out work after marriage.** Are you staying on the job? You can't plan autonomously anymore. Marriage is a union of economics and lifestyles as much as a union of hearts. Work decisions are ultimately personal, but the more you and your partner understand and accept prior to the merger, the better. For example, unlike many women of Mom's generation, you can't assume staying home is okay with your husband. He may have his own "liberated" ideas about spousal roles and expect you to carry your share of the weight from Day One. Together, consider your occupational goals, lifestyle preferences and financial needs and objectives. Then determine the right job decisions for *both* of you.

• **Quitting the rat race? Apologize to no one!** Not to your coworkers nor to your liberated friends. Bowing out of the game may feel lousy at first, especially if you're winning. But sooner than you may expect, you'll probably be grateful to be on the sidelines—clean, healed, and rested. If you find you miss the thick of things, however, don't hesitate to admit it to yourself. Seek a way back. In fact, prior to leaving your job, it doesn't hurt to ask your boss if he or she would give you some consideration should you ever want to return.

• **Negotiate a work adjustment.** Maybe you'd like to keep your job, but differently—with flexible hours, with limited travel, on a consulting basis, from home, from overseas, whatever. Be rational and politic in your proposal. Anticipate specific points of boss hesitation, and have counterarguments at the ready.

• **Muster the energy to look for that new job in the new place.** For starters, knock that pessimistic look off your face. You know more people than you did early in your career. And as the world grows smaller, their contacts probably extend farther afield. Work those contacts—yours, your groom's, your friends', your former coworkers', your new neighbors' and the contacts of the woman at the bank who opened your new account. First impressions are mainly about superficiality, unfortunately, so arm yourself with a modern—but not juvenile—hairstyle and interview outfit. Transmit experience versus age. Hurry up and wait, as the saying goes. Check the mirror for pessimism every day.

• **Travel a new path.** As a bride, you're in a transitional frame of mind anyway. Consider going down a different career path that's always beckoned you. Get some training or accept a developmental position with lower pay, if need be, to make the transition.

• **Hang out that shingle.** Those of you who've ever considered self-employment might take this opportunity to open that antiques shop or import tropical produce. By now, you may have accumulated adequate savings to invest in your venture. And for the first time, you're about to have another source of income and benefits to lean on as you wait for those ventures to show a profit. There's no shame in leaning for a time.

That Other Marriage Contract: Prenups, Wills, and "Legalese"

P art of me envies my friend Gloria, eight years my junior and, in marriage, my older and wiser sister by an eternity. She and her husband married right out of college. Funny, how marriage became "in" again among 20-somethings by the end of the '70s.

The point is, Gloria's marriage started with nothing. That's not easy, but it sure is simple.

Because the "marital contract" isn't merely a spiritual notion. It also means legalities and paperwork. It's unromantic. It adds to the meetings, decisions, negotiations, and documents already heaped upon our lives. It relates mainly to the *demise* of marriage, via death or divorce. And with age, the process only compounds. Unlike Gloria, we mid-lifers tend to enter marriage not only with our hearts and minds, but also with complex financial profiles. Be they strong or shaky, our profiles have grown large over time.

But no whining! On balance, most mid-lifers are fortunate to be launching marriages with more than, say, a rusted car and an unpaid student loan. You likely have some resources to work with. Therefore, you have nothing to be concerned about, except maybe prenuptial agreements, wills, trusts, investments, transfers of real property, taxes, preservation of capital, pensions, living wills, powers of attorney, insurance coverage. . . .

Keep repeating: *I am fortunate. I am fortunate. . . .*

While younger couples make plans for first homes or first babies, you may be thinking ahead to retirement, long-term care, providing for heirs, and maybe even the disposal of your remains. Mid-lifers focus on these long-term issues as they begin to realize their term isn't as long as it used to be. Some of us have grappled with these issues as they relate to elderly parents and relatives. Among our own generation, many of us know people who've wound up in early retirement, divorced or with a long-term disability. After a while, the concept of estate planning begins to sound less high-brow and more like the necessity it is for commoners and blue bloods alike. You might not have all your plans and directives in order yet, but at least you know you should.

Now it's time for you to reexamine your plans in the context of marriage. Much of this business can wait until (shortly) after the honeymoon. But at least two matters are best resolved before the wedding day: prenups, for obvious reason, and wills. On issues of inheritance, the two documents are closely linked and should therefore be considered simultaneously. You may save lawyer time and fees that way, too. On the downside, thinking about these two documents at the same time can scramble the brain:

Why did we agree that my life insurance should go to you?
Because you're dead.

WILLS

Like most major life events, adding a spouse is cause for reviewing and probably revising your will. Certain procrastinating mid-lifers need to do wills for the first time. We have our reasons, if not excuses, for dawdling.

Namely: Leave our worldly possessions to *whom*?

Regardless of age, it's entirely common for single people without kids to have neither a will nor life insurance. I evaded the question all my adult life. Besides a cat and some stringy plants, I had no dependents. Nor had I siblings, nieces or nephews. My parents' income was secured for the rest of their lives. Other relations: They're so many, I've never known where to begin.

"If you don't have a will, who's going to pay for your funeral?" my mother asked when I was in my twenties. Do wills cover that? News to me. Well, I already had Mom named as beneficiary on my life insurance at work. That ought to cover a plain-vanilla funeral, I figured. Years later, though I still had no dependents, I'd slowly accumulated other baggage. After my funeral, there'd be other liabilities. And assets left over. If I didn't earmark who gets what, some judge would do so. No! So I'd better do a will . . . one of these days.

According to Joan Wilbon, a knowledgeable Washington attorney, there's nothing like an impending wedding to get procrastinators in gear. Our assets have no marching orders, and now they're at risk of getting further confused in matrimony.

In these so-called "United" States, there are variations on this theme, but *generally speaking*, here's what happens to your stuff when you die: Any property you own jointly will pass to the other owner. If you have funds in a custodial account for a minor, that account continues to be held until the minor reaches legal age. On life insurance plans, company savings plans or other benefits, the beneficiary you named gets the proceeds.

Everything else you've got is distributed according to your wishes as expressed in your will. If you want your property divided between Future Husband and existing children, fine, and you can specify who gets what. If you want all your property to go to your alma mater or ex-boyfriend, that's fine, too.

There's another inevitable heir: Uncle Sam, the guy who taxes your money when you earn it, when you save it and again when you leave it behind. There are plenty of strategies for minimizing his take from your estate. The first strategy is dumb luck: A large chunk of your estate is automatically sheltered from taxes by the Internal Revenue Service. And that chunk is growing. In 1997, it was $600,000. By 2006, it will be a cool million bucks. The second strategy is getting married:

There's no federal tax on any portion of your estate that you direct to your new husband.

Once I faced up to it, the will cracked more easily than I'd expected. I provided for my parents, in case they outlive me. If they live way past their life expectancy, who knows how far their own money will go? For other people and charities I care about, I gave the executor guidelines for the selection of beneficiaries, along with a few specific, non-binding recommendations. Granted, the executor's job won't be easy.

At my lawyer's prompting, I also spelled out a living will—the circumstances under which someone may "pull my plug"—and a basic directive for my disposal. Here I was, in the heady days at the dawn of my new life, planning the grim end of it all. But it was a good thing, disclosing preferences with Future Husband right then and there. After all, something could happen to one of us on our honeymoon.

Choice of executor for my will was my biggest quandary. I had no dependent to choose. Future Husband? A hell of a wedding present to give him. Relatives? The most dependable are older than I am; who knows if they'll be around when I'm gone? So far, the executor is my mother. Eventually, I'll probably have to select another. Future Husband, brace yourself.

Deciding how to distribute your property requires that you're clear about what property is yours. This is relatively easy for singles who may own all their property outright. After marriage, however, the concept of "yours" may grow cloudy. For me, light dawned when I sold my condominium. When I bought the place, I didn't even know Future Husband. My name alone was on the title and the mortgage. I alone made the payments and paid taxes. I alone paid for every expense, from the bathroom upgrade to shelf paper. When the apartment was sold, guess who else had to approve the sale? It was simpler for me to have him sign the papers and be done with it than to stand on principle and prove he didn't have to approve. I was annoyed nonetheless.

Rules of property in marriage have countless variations. Chief among them is the concept of "community property"—a Spanish colonial tradition that survives in nine states, mainly in the West. Community property laws pretty much say: What was yours *before* marriage is yours and remains so. What becomes yours during marriage is yours *and* his, 50–50. That's regardless of whose name may be on the deed, the sales receipt or the bank statement. That's also regardless of who worked herself to the bone to acquire the property while the other one snoozed on the sofa.

In most other states, laws governing marital property are more basic: An asset generally belongs to whomever's name is on it, individually or jointly. Gloria and her husband, the couple who started out with barely a dime, are awash in dimes, real estate, stock options and other assets some 20 years later. Being childless, they're just getting around to preparing wills. She wants to provide for her relations; he wants to provide for his. The rub is: Virtually all their assets are in both their names. Couples like these, and there are probably zillions, often have to craft carefully worded wills or trust funds to clarify whose assets are whose to leave to whomever.

Property is never more fraught with complication than in a divorce. If you've ever divorced or even heard a tale of divorce east of the Rockies, you know this well. Couples generally have to divide property "equally," a term that's open to wide interpretation in most states. In a noncommunity-property state, that means figuring out, and maybe proving, that the four-wheel drive or the toaster is yours, his or jointly owned (and, if so, in what proportions).

This is just one of the compelling reasons more couples of all ages are doing. . . .

PRENUPS

In a television interview some years back, Bette Midler sang praises supreme for her new husband, an apparent love for all time.

"So there's no need for a prenuptial agreement?" asked the devilish reporter.

"Let's not go too far," said Midler.

Prenups aren't just for the rich and famous. Nor are they just for mid-lifers. Mid-lifers, however, have more at stake, and we may have different goals for our prenups.

Given the rising rates of divorce and remarriage, it's not surprising that prenups have become commonplace over the past 20 years. Still, I was surprised to find my prenup was on more minds than two.

My friend Darlene, whispering in the movies: "You *are* doing a prenup, aren't you?"

My mother, an old-school woman of the pre-prenup days: "I think it would be a good idea if you talked to him about a prenuptial agreement."

Another friend asked: (a) Did we do a prenup? (b) What was in it?

I thought Future Husband had charmed the women in my life. Did they eye him instead as a deadbeat? It was smart for *me* to want a prenup, but it hurt my feelings that *they* wanted me to have one.

What is this prenup anyway, and why does it seem to make everyone sigh with relief?

There's the occasional prenup that spells out marital roles and responsibilities: who works, who cooks, who pays the bills, who mows the lawn. Some agreements even dictate frequency of sex or maximum weight gain, though no court in the land wants to come near such cases. However, most prenups focus on who gets what assets in the event of divorce. In addition, mid-lifers and senior citizens often reinforce inheritance rights, even if spelled out in their wills, to ensure that children or other loved ones don't get the shaft.

A prenup can't swindle you into getting less than your due under the law. However, it can allow you to be generous if you want—for example, by transferring individually owned property to joint ownership. A prenup can also spell out specific agreements, such as who gets the Persian rug in his or her half of the assets upon divorce. And who's more inclined to be agreeable: a loving couple on the threshhold of matrimony or a bitter couple in the throes of divorce? Hence, the prenup.

According to Joan the lawyer, the people most likely to want prenups (a) have assets, (b) have worked long and hard to get those assets, and (c) have children they want those assets to go to. Increasingly, they're likely to be women—the "Murphy Browns," as Joan calls them—whose assets are the spoils of hard-driving careers. In prenup negotiations, they're tough and they're frugal.

Their mantra: *He gets me, and that's all he gets.*

Valerie, a training consultant, marched into the den one day and blurted to her husband-to-be: "I want a prenup, and I want to keep my own name."

"Okay," he calmly replied.

Though Valerie's hardly a bashful person, she had evaded mention of the "p" word for a considerable time. The term has a hostile ring to it. Yet, unlike marriage, a prenup is impossible to propose gradually or subtly without sounding like you're up to something dastardly. I was spared the discomfort of making the overture by Future Husband: "I believe our love is good for a lifetime," he began, "but I've been through a divorce. I'm not naive. . . ."

Fortunately, you don't need to execute a long windup before the pitch to a fellow mid-lifer. Most mid-lifers grasp prenup wisdom readily and dispassionately. Most wise are the divorced, for even amicable divorces have been made difficult for lack of a preconceived plan. Lifelong singles have gained at least a smidgen of wisdom looking at (1) our friends' divorces and (2) all the stuff, for better and for worse, in our own economic baggage and his.

Discussing your prenup goals, one-on-one, goes easier if you keep this in mind: A prenup isn't simply about self-defense, much less vengeance lurking in the shadows. A prenup can also be one of the ways you assure your partner that you have *his* interests at heart.

As much as a prenup can say . . .

- *I retain full ownership of my business* or

- *That home equity debt is on you, sweetie* or

- *That inheritance I expect to get in the future is mine, all mine*

. . . it can also say . . .

- *I won't diminish the inheritance due your kids* or

- *I'm not marrying you for your stock options* or

- *Should we divorce, you'll never find me across the table from you at a shareholder meeting of your family's business.*

In other words, a prenup can express *You can trust me,* not just *I don't trust you.* It can also ease the qualms of other interested parties—heirs, benefactors or business partners—should you choose to confide relevant aspects of the prenup to them.

I plight thee my troth are just words at the altar. The assurances you give in a prenup, on the other hand, are binding—as binding as Edward the VIII abdicating the throne for the woman he loved. Yes, with a stretch of imagination, prenups are nearly romantic.

My prenup chat with Future Husband didn't take long. Perhaps like other mid-lifers, both of us already had clear ideas about what we cared about and what we didn't. Fortunately, those ideas were compatible. Call me idealistic, but I believe when two people care about each other, they also care about—or at least tolerate—each other's interests.

I had no interest in alimony, as either taker or giver. In principle, if not always in fact, alimony is not tantamount to punitive damages. Rather, it's intended to "rehabilitate" a dependent spouse to a point where he or she can become self-supporting. And in my case, if I could make a living for 23 years all by myself, who am I to suggest that I couldn't and shouldn't continue to do so? I hear some voices—female voices—saying *Get off your high horse, honey.* Sorry, Ivana, that's where I sit. My only special request was a share of Future Husband's pension. Quitting my job for the sake of *whither thou goest* meant giving up pension eligibility. My "employer" in my home-based business offers me no pension plan. And at my age, if I were to begin working for someone else again, I'd have little chance of qualifying for a meaningful pension.

By the time we got to Joan's office, we were both pretty darn lighthearted about the whole prenup business.

"Uh-oh, a woman," Future Husband joked. "I don't stand a chance." I took comfort in her age, which was in the same ballpark as ours.

Taking wisdom from lawyers, doctors, or other professionals who could pass for teenagers is still weird to me.

Be forewarned: Prenups are largely about confession. To ensure the agreement is legally binding, all financial truths must be laid bare. You stand naked, cellulite and all, before your partner and some lawyer. For mid-life singles forever accustomed to privacy, this can be especially awkward. You may already have come a long way, sharing with your partner the pain of a past love affair or childhood bed-wetting. Now you're exposing your most private part of all—money!—and you may have an embarrassment of riches, deficit, or mismanagement. He finds out you earn a bigger salary than he does! You find out all his money is invested in a seaside resort in Kansas! He finds out you've got thousands of dollars idling in interest-free checking! You find out how much alimony he pays!

Says Joan, however, mid-lifers are rarely bug-eyed with amazement at these revelations. "They're more sensitive than younger couples to each other's values and habits."

Joan further observes about mid-lifers:

- You're easier to work with than younger couples. For starters, you and your partner have discussed your prenup goals, at least generally, before you arrive at the lawyer's office.

- Mid-life prenups are more complicated and time-consuming to prepare, covering more assets, more debts, sometimes business interests, sometimes children.

- Neither party's reluctant to be there. However, some people— usually men—are reluctant to tell all about their finances. Or they may quietly transfer assets to children or other parties in advance. That's perfectly legal and often smart, but it's perfectly *illegal* to keep it a secret.

"I'll leave you two alone to read and talk it over," said Joan, closing the door to the conference room as Future Husband and I faced the prenup in writing. The convivial chat of our last meeting had been transformed into a document—thick, stern, legal and cold. Attached to the back were our financial confessions, now known as "exhibits." How pertinent. I was heartened to find the occasional clause of reassurance:

While the parties contemplate a long and lasting marriage . . . they ain't crazy.

Each of the parties believes that their marriage will be strengthened by the establishment of . . . some heavy, steel handcuffs about one another's wrists.

"How was it?" Joan asked of my prenup-and-will experience, when all was said and signed. Not bad at all for a mind-bending process concerning divorce, disability, and death. Maybe that's because I felt I'd planned for my immortality even as I'd planned for my demise. Then again, maybe it's because I turned the process into a sort of movie—an out-of-body drama, where I merely acted the part of the scrutinizing divorcée or deathbed diva. Or maybe the process helped drive home the beauty of no longer being alone. Future Husband and I are there for each other—for richer, for poorer, in sickness and in health, until and *after* death do us part—and, strangest of all, in the event of divorce.

On Prenups and Wills . . . Consider This

• **Consult a lawyer.** This book does *not* constitute legal advice. Seek an attorney who specializes in estate law about arrangements that best fit your needs and wants as an individual and as a couple. Your lawyer should be licensed and experienced in the state where you expect to reside at the start of your marriage.

• **Never move to another state, let alone another country.** Just kidding. Since you might indeed move around in this age of mobility, see if your lawyer can draft your prenup, will and/or trust documents in a way that makes the provisions as transferable as possible. Otherwise, you may have to review and revise your will, at least, every time you make a move.

• **Don't wait until the last minute.** These issues should be considered with as little time pressure as possible. Start the process at least three months in advance or whenever you know you're getting married—whichever comes later.

• **If you're childless, think up alternate beneficiaries.** Consider your husband, parents, other relatives, godchildren, alma mater or favorite charities.

• **Write your will as if you'll die tomorrow.** Don't worry about the unborn, the house you haven't built yet or older heirs who may predecease you. Periodically review your will and revise it whenever your circumstances change significantly. Adding a codicil, or amendment, is sufficient in many cases and less costly than a full overhaul.

• **Make a prenup decision.** Whether or not to do one depends on your circumstances. If you're a mid-lifer, you've probably got baggage, and that's circumstance aplenty.

• **Broach the prenup subject directly.** Start with a positive statement, such as: "I want to be with you forever." Or "I think we should protect *each other* in the event. . . ."

• **Talk with your partner before you talk with the lawyer.** Discuss your respective goals for a prenup before you get to the law office, where the meter ticks. Time is money!

• **Consult web sites and reference books.** You can minimize the lawyer's time and invoice further by doing some research on prenups and wills on your own. Some references include questionnaires and worksheets that can help you put your interests in perspective. They'll prompt you to address important issues you might not have considered. Don't bypass legal counsel, however. One wrong word in a self-written document could jeopardize your intentions.

• **Check tax implications.** The answer to who-gets-what should not be Uncle Sam. For both your will and prenup, find out what income or estate tax liabilities exist—both federal and state—for yourself and your survivors. Either you or your lawyer should consult an astute tax attorney before finalizing your documents.

• **Don't be hasty.** Mid-lifers value expediency. Just don't cross the line and rush into things. Don't be conciliatory just to get things over with. Don't scan the documents; scrutinize. *Please* don't be hasty because you think you're so mature and wise that divorce is out of the question and this is just an exercise.

• **Of course, leave attitude out of the discussion.** Anticipate any differences of opinion. Be prepared to explain your point of view rationally, and give his viewpoint a fair hearing in return. Trust that you'll reach consensus.

• **Get naked together, financially.** Divulge assets, debts, income. Not only must you include this information in your prenup document; the revelations will also trigger constructive discussion about money management after marriage.

• **Keep prior assets in your own individual name.** Once you're married, you're free to transfer some premarital assets, such as savings or property, into joint assets if you're fool enough—I mean, generous enough—to want to do so. But as a general rule, keep your separate premarital assets in your name alone. That makes who-owns-what a whole lot clearer in the event of death or divorce.

• **Get dual representation.** You and your partner can draft the prenup with one lawyer, but the final document should be reviewed and endorsed by *two*—one lawyer on your behalf, one on his. In some states, this is absolutely required.

• **Be as open or as close-mouthed as you want to be.**
Don't be surprised if people ask if you have a prenup. It's
become so commonplace, it's no cause for shame or raised
eyebrows anymore. Yet it's still no one's business but yours.

~

Mrs. Confused:
The Name Game

It's 48 hours till the moment of truth, and we're at Village Hall—a quarter-century-old building that didn't exist when I escaped the village to go to college. Now we're in the office of the Village Clerk, being assisted by an intern who's about to graduate from my high school some 30 years after my own commencement. Like nothing else, a hometown visit makes the returning wayfarer feel ancient.

Well, this one-page application for a marriage license should be a breeze. Future Husband remembered his passport and divorce papers. I even know the name of the small Florida town where my father was born. But I'm stumped at the second line.

Surname after marriage: _____

I knew I had to decide sometime. It hadn't dawned on me that time would be now.

Today's brides have unlimited surname options—maiden name, husband's name, previous husband's name, combinations of any of the above.

First-time brides have lived forever with their original names (let's outlaw "maiden" names). Whether our lives have lasted two decades or five, dropping the only name we've ever known feels strange.

The longer you've lived with a name, the better known it is to the rest of the world. Therein lie the complications. Not only do *you* know yourself as Jane Doe; you're also Jane Doe to: Social Security, banks, the Postal Service, investment firms, insurance companies, creditors, credit bureaus, the IRS, Passport Administration, lawyers who draw up deeds and wills, issuers of licenses and diplomas, frequent flyer programs, the company you work for, the Board of Elections, the video rental store and on and on. Over time, documentation breeds. This quandary holds true for lifelong singles as well as for the divorced who've been known most of their lives by the name of their previous husband.

Maybe a few brides stick with their old names just to avoid the nightmare of fixing endless documents. For most, however, the decision rests on a blend of practicality, pride and sentiment.

Not long after I was engaged, I began pondering what name to use at work. In the process, I discovered that more than a few people in my company were wed clandestinely—to other employees.

"You know Jane Smith in Legal and John Brown in Marketing? They're married."

You're kidding!

"Then there's Steve Jones in Finance and Joyce Grant in Human Resources. . . ."

Steve and Joyce?? No!!

"Yep. Joyce used to be married to Bob Thornton in Technical Computing. . . ."

Thanks to separate names and a sprawling workforce, only a handful of close associates knew the private business of these people. I liked that a lot.

A wise female colleague pointed out: "You have *equity* in your old name." She was darn right! I'd amassed a quarter-century of hard work, achievement, mistakes, headaches, satisfaction, stab wounds, growth and mostly good reputation under that name. Future Husband didn't have a thing to do with it, nor did his ancestors. And come to think of it, maybe *my* ancestors did.

Equity was especially important, now that I was about to put out my own shingle. Business cards would look pretty silly with the footnote "formerly known as. . . ."

On the personal side, we're proud of the bloodlines our original name represents, even if it identifies only our father's half of the family tree. We're not being transferred from one fold to another, complete with goats to compensate our new owner for his trouble. Nonetheless, some of us mid-lifers have a toehold on the era of our formative years, when women assumed their husbands' names, period. Whenever we preteenagers got a crush on a boy, the first order of business was to attach our first name to our what-if surname and try it on. Not a hyphenated surname; just *his* surname. We privately whispered it. We wrote it in our diaries and looseleaf notebooks. In print. In script. In pencil. In Magic Marker. With "Mrs." and without. ("Ms." didn't exist.) The name thing was critical to our concept of marriage. One of my crushes withered as soon as I realized how foolish my first name sounded with the last name Bell.

Now we first-timers finally get a chance to see and hear our names next to the names of husbands for the first time. We like this! As a 70-year-old newlywed, Aunt Bern glowed perceptibly when addressed as Mrs. Johnson instead of Miss or Ms. Spigner. In her case, "Mrs." not only signified respect for her lawful connection to the man she loved; it also rid her of the "old maid" stigma. Fortunately, subsequent generations of women have put that stigma in its rightful grave.

Second-time newlyweds may have recovered from this pubescent obsession the first time around. They may have already suffered through administrative and emotional withdrawal from one man's name, and they may be less than eager to change their name again. Many a modern senior citizen who remarries sticks with the name of her first husband. It may represent 50 years' worth of data, social recognition and personal habit. Moreover, the senior bride is often a widow rather than a divorcée. Though she's found new love, she hasn't lost respect for the old name or the man it belonged to.

Bern, incidentally, kept Spigner or Spigner-Johnson on many documents—Medicare, for example—to avoid being confused with thousands of other Bernice Johnsons out there. That's one of the practical factors that may influence your choice of name. Or you might pick your name based on ease of pronunciation or spelling. My friend Anne was delighted to assume her new husband's plain name after a lifetime of correcting people on her original tongue-twister.

The bride will retain her name. In today's published wedding announcements, this sentence has become commonplace. But no matter how passionate and true, couples with two independent surnames sound more like a law partnership than a marriage to many of us molded in the day of Ozzie and Harriet Nelson. We're fully conscious of the inherent sexism in taking a man's name. Still, we want our marriage to sound and feel like family, with a single common denominator.

Even more old-fashioned are our elders. If we assume any name besides our new husband's, our parents may find it silly. Some may even be hostile to the idea. Elaine's father insists on addressing letters to her in her husband's name. He hasn't forgotten that she kept her own name, she says. He just disapproves, and he persists out of protest.

Having the groom take *our* surname may be too avant-garde for most mid-lifers, in spite of our cheers for equal rights. However, I'll be delighted if twenty-first-century applications for marriage licenses question *his* surname, for a change, as well as ours. One recent newspaper announcement stated *Mr. S* _____ *will change his name.* That's incomplete information, but I think we can presume he didn't switch to the Artist Formerly Known as Prince. "What a wimp," Future Husband half-joked.

A bit more commonly, some liberated couples combine their names to make both parties Smith-Jones, for example. Political correctness aside, I pity the future great-grandchildren who may have to haul around eight names. In a variation on this theme, my coworker took his new wife's surname as his middle name. He wanted to feel connected in name to her son, whom he adopted, without making the son abandon the surname he'd known for all his nine years.

Names are overwhelmingly personal, and choosing one (or two) should be entirely up to you. Just the same, find out if your partner has an opinion. When asked, Future Husband essentially shrugged. "Use whatever name you feel most comfortable with." Though his answer was "correct," it momentarily disappointed. He didn't give a hoot whether I shared his name or not. I bet Ozzie Nelson would have cared.

Dual surnames have been an excellent and popular compromise since our liberation days of the '70's. Indeed, most of my friends who married back then chose to be "hyphenated." Today, they rarely bother with their original names, just to make life easier. And indeed, some dual surnames are cumbersome. I can't help feeling annoyed when a woman insists on being verbally addressed at all times as, say, Ms. Spaghettini-DeGustibus—unless she's a tennis pro, in which case, it's cool. Some women go ballistic if a hyphen has been dropped or added.

My surname joined with Future Husband's wouldn't make a ten-worst list, but it would hardly be as concise or rhythmic as "Mary Tyler Moore." I therefore chose to choose one name or the other. But which? Fear of commitment cuts a wide course.

"As long as you don't join the two names with a hyphen," advised the very patient Village Clerk, "you can legally use either your maiden name or husband's name, alone or together." Perfect! I filled the blank with Future Husband's surname. My original name became my middle name. Now I could have my old identity in business, my new identity everywhere else, both identities if and whenever useful. I could waffle for a lifetime.

On the Name Game . . .
Consider This

• **Make up your mind about your name *before* you get to City Hall.** Discuss your preference with your partner in advance; don't surprise him in a public office.

• **Try out all your name options verbally and on paper.** Regress to junior high. Beyond the three p's—principle, pride and practicality—your name should feel good, too. You'll be wearing it every day.

• **Use your original name or a hyphenated name at work.** It's especially practical at a large company. Otherwise, colleagues will be stumped for months. *Sally Sloan? Who's that?* Maybe you'll get your memos and phone calls; maybe you won't. Keeping your original name will also remind any doubters that you're still "you," as committed to your job as before.

• **If you're looking for a new job after marriage, use your old name.** If you're starting a *new* job after marriage, starting it with a brand-new name won't confuse anyone. If you're still looking for a new job, stick with the name that's known to former employers, schools, licensing agencies and other references.

• **Ignore anyone who doesn't like your name.** If anyone besides you feels your name is awkward, socially inappropriate or politically incorrect, that's their problem. Besides, they'll get used to your name sooner than they think.

• **On official documents, use your full legal name, per your marriage license.** That includes contracts, insurance policies, tax returns and the like.

• **If your legal name is new or altered, notify official agencies.** At minimum, make sure you cover the Social Security Administration, the Passport Office and the Internal Revenue Service. Since many institutions require a copy of your marriage license to make changes, you can't do much in advance of the wedding. Afterward, take care of business sooner rather than later. Some institutions may insist on seeing your original license with the seal.

• **Expect confusion.** If you choose alternate names—one for work, one for all else—even *you'll* get confused once in a while. *What do you mean, you have no reservation in my name?* But you can make the juggling act work. Maintain some form of identification in each name. Be consistent where it counts.

PART TWO

So You Can't Forget the Wedding

~

Attitudes: Getting Ready to Get Ready

When's the big day?

My dental hygienist: "Well, I wanted to get married in December you should see how beautiful our church is at Christmastime poinsettias everywhere and besides we'd save so much money on flowers but my sister just got married in June so my mother said please let's wait until next year so now we're planning our wedding for March we were going to go to New York for our honeymoon but if we were going to do New York I only wanted to do it first class do you know how much it costs to book a suite at the Plaza overlooking Central Park for that kind of money I'd rather go to Cancun or someplace like that and lie on the beach."

My manicurist: "In two years when my fiancé finishes college he wants to get married in North Carolina that's where he's from but I want to do it here in Texas where *I'm* from and so does my Mom so that's where it's going to be this is his second marriage he already had a chance to have a wedding his way now it's my turn."

An administrative assistant: "I want to get married the Saturday after Thanksgiving but my cousin just announced the same date for her wedding do you think I should ask her to postpone it after all I got engaged before she did it seems only fair. . . ."

My former supervisor: "I dunno. Maybe in the spring."

Quiz: Which of these women was *not* in her twenties?

Sure, you want your marital kickoff to be special. You're as romantic and fanciful as the younger bride. But you also want to keep the wedding in perspective. There's already quite enough going on in your life: The downstairs neighbor may be suing you for water damage. The IRS may be auditing your tax return. The big presentation to the prospective client is coming up. You're trying to talk Dad into cataract surgery. Now you're preparing for marriage, too—merging habitats and habits, negotiating prenups and reassuring relatives, bosses and pets.

On top of all that, do you strive to invest months of aggravation and stress in a three-hour event? I don't think so. It's a cost-benefit thing.

What constitutes wedding aggravation and stress varies widely among us. You may have no patience for anything beyond a quick trip to City Hall during your lunch hour. On the other hand, your limits may reach as high as 500 guests and the New York Philharmonic Orchestra on a private island in the Bahamas. The point is, every mature woman knows that some joyful ideas can be hell to execute. You know your personal tolerance for hell, and you're not going to sentence yourself to hell voluntarily. After all, if your wedding's going to be hell, why bother?

While brides of any age aim for flawless execution, mid-life brides don't expect to die at the first sign of a mishap. Nor do we obsess about doing things right, according to some dubious protocol. "Right" is very important to young brides, and it may be the fastest track to Wedding Hell there is. Just read the letters to the editor of any bridal magazine or Web site. Most read something like: *Is it okay if I—*

- *Invite one college roommate but not the other?*

- *Include my friend Julia in the wedding party, even though she'll be eight months pregnant?*

- *Turn down Uncle Sid's offer to play the accordion during the ceremony?*

- *Seat my divorced parents at the same table?*

Yes, whatever! It's *your* wedding! Yet some young brides will consult everyone they know and second-guess themselves repeatedly. Midlife brides share many of the same issues, but we're not going to sweat them. We haven't the time or patience. We put faith in our common sense and courtesy, and we know lightning won't strike, should we make a faux pas. We'll make executive decisions; soothe the offended, if need be, and move on.

"Older brides are less nervous about their weddings," said a makeup artist who's put the blush on brides young and old. "Older brides know 'shit happens.' "

"At your own wedding," Barbra Streisand told *People*, "you really can't make a mistake."

LET THE GAMES BEGIN

I tried my hand at knitting once. Choosing a pattern was fun. Choosing the yarn was fun. Envisioning the finished product on my back was fun. Even learning the stitches was fun. But the knitting was plain drudgery. That's how I felt about the prospect of planning my wedding. I didn't know how to do it. I didn't particularly want to do it. I just wanted it to be—and be wonderful. I'm probably not alone in this feeling, but I don't claim to be typical of brides of my generation or any other.

A wedding is a "special event," which is a sugar-coated term for work, if you're the one who has to make it happen. During my career, I've occasionally been sentenced to planning special events, and I hate this call of duty right down to those teeny envelopes for reply cards. Don't get me started on seating charts.

So I procrastinated. My excuses were worthy. During the six months between engagement and wedding: I was doing the work of three people in a recently downsized office. I was fixing up my apartment to prepare it for sale. I was devoting as many weekends as possible to visiting long-distance Future Husband. I was cleaning out Aunt Bern's apartment; she passed away before I got the chance to tell her I was engaged. I was genuinely preoccupied. But fundamentally I was in denial.

Eventually, curiosity impelled me to find out the basics. I called Village Hall in my hometown and got directed to the Village Clerk:

"How does one get married?" I inquired.

At least in New York State, the elements were pretty straightforward: an application, a deadline, some identification, 15 bucks, a 48-hour waiting period (to sober up?), an officiant, and a couple of witnesses. Qualifying for matrimony is pretty lightweight stuff, I discovered. Try to get a license to drive a car or cut hair this easily. Yet marriage is arguably the most profound transaction of our lives. That's all the more reason maturity comes in handy: We'd better know what we're doing, because there's no road test or board of examiners to confirm we're worthy. I guess that's because we're not likely to injure anyone besides ourselves.

Thank goodness *one* aspect of getting married is easy. But on to the rest. . . .

Every mid-life bride is of course an individual. In many ways, we're also like brides of any age. Still, according to wedding consultants and vendors of every stripe, mid-life brides have some common, distinguishing marks. We generally:

- Make plans with our grooms

- Make plans without our mothers

- Do things at the last minute

- Are more decisive

- Go for the nontraditional (in invitations, ceremonies, receptions, etc.)

- Spend our own money—and more of it

- Have more fun.

Though we don't obsess about our weddings overall, my friend Tess observes that busy mid-lifers selectively focus on One Perfect Thing. We have neither the time nor the patience to worry everything to the max. But we will get nutty over one element that's of special personal interest—the dress, the flowers, the music, whatever.

"Buy a good wedding planner," my experienced friend Greta advised.

You can *buy* these people? Oh, she meant one of those how-to manuals. With tremendous reluctance and attitude, I visited the wedding section of a mega-bookstore. Towering shelves groaned under the weight of myriad guides on weddings—traditional weddings, avant-garde weddings, interfaith weddings, gay weddings, weddings tailored to specific ethnic groups, wedding vows, wedding dresses, wedding flowers, wedding showers, wedding cakes, wedding music, wedding stationery and on and on.

A really big category is wedding etiquette—the bibles of doing things "right." Even after flipping through a table of contents or two, I failed to get it. It seemed to me that the social basics we learned in childhood—*please, thank you, sorry*—were plenty good enough for weddings.

The grandmothers of wedding books are the thick, all-inclusive "workbooks" with timetables and infinite checklists of marching orders. One book's timetable started two years in advance of the wedding date. *Two years.* That's fine for a bridge expansion. Or for a young bride whose mother *must* book the Colonnade Room, or some such. But mid-life couples, once engaged, want a more timely trip to the altar. That holds true even for couples who've been together for a decade or more. It's not that we're pregnant or near death's door. It's just that once we've decided to be married, we want to get on with it.

"He asked, and we're doing it," said a breathless 40-something customer in a bridal shop, looking for something off the rack that she could wear down the aisle a month later.

Mid-life brides aim to do weddings the way they aim to do most things in life—efficiently—even if we wind up doing them hastily. This approach can work because, no matter how desirable we, too, may find the Colonnade Room or the must-have soloist, it's not *important*. We're flexible on just about every wedding detail other than choice of groom.

Do wedding planners need to tell us mid-lifers what to do as if we were children? Okay, that's half right. A wedding has its own nuances, distinct from other projects, which means we can indeed use some guidance on the particulars, especially if we're first-timers. We can also use an occasional kick in the butt to nudge us out of procrastination.

On the downside, wedding planners tend to forget that we're quite grown. We've renovated kitchens, raised children, or engineered corporate takeovers. We know a thing or two about planning, decision-making, budgeting, negotiating, scheduling, and supervising. Experience tells us, for example, to look at samples of the photographer's work, to get the caterer's estimate in writing and to get references and contracts for everything.

I bought the least intimidating, patronizing and dictatorial workbook I could find—sort of a time manager in light-but-not-baby blue. Even when closed, its very presence prodded me into taking care of business. The checklist was refreshingly minimalist; it didn't stage a hostile take-over of my life. And like a crossword-puzzle solver, I felt accomplished each time I filled in a blank.

As my plans unfolded, I had a neat revelation: Though I'd never in my life "thought" about my wedding—never consciously scripted or rehearsed My Wedding Day—nuggets of ideas sprang forth, fully formed, from some remote sub-basement of my brain. It was as if some Wedding Elves had been hiding there for decades, waiting patiently for the Big Mo, smirking as I meandered through bachelorhood, oblivious to my future.

On Getting Ready . . .
Consider This

• **Keep sight of where you've drawn the line between wedding joy and wedding hell at all times.**

• **Use a wedding planner.** Don't think you're too wise and mature; get one. Even if you've had a previous wedding or two, it's not so routine that you can do it blindfolded. Today, there are software planners as well as traditional printed manuals. Try to choose a planner that's concise and that doesn't talk to you as if you're a grown-up-in-training. You can invent your own planner, structuring to-do lists and timetables the way you want them. But you may find it easier to take a planner off the shelf and adapt it.

• **Don't procrastinate.** You probably have a short time frame between knowing you're getting married and doing it. The wedding isn't the only thing happening in your life, but it's not the least important thing, either. Putting preparations off till the last minute will only increase stress. Do you need it?

• **Don't be hasty, either.** Remind yourself constantly that there's a difference between getting things done efficiently and getting them done hastily. Haste can cost you time, trouble, money and/or dissatisfaction.

• **Summon your Wedding Elves.** On every decision, from choice of vows to choice of dress: Close your eyes. See if any hidden wedding fantasies rise to the frontal lobe.

~

Coors Light or Candlelight?: Matters of Style

In the summer of '49, two young first-timers exchanged their vows at sunset on Jones Beach. Their ceremony was a secret, known only to the few others present—the minister, the maid of honor and the best man. My father promised my mother that if he dropped the ring in the sand, she'd have to look for it.

I particularly relished this tale in the '60's. Before they succumbed to bourgeois respectability, my parents were actually hip.

In the 80s, not long after Aunt Bern hinted at wedding plans of her own, she went ahead and did it—quietly, privately, furtively. Proper Bern had her ceremony in a church rather than in the sand. But the point is, her wedding was small and discreet, just like my mother's. That's been the case for most of the rest of her side of my family, too. Maybe it's in the genes.

That's how I'd do my wedding, too—small, discreet, simple. As a teen, I envisioned elopement one day.

Hi Mom, what's new?

Oh, nothing. What's new with you?

Not much. I just broke a fingernail. Oh, and I got married yesterday.

I doubt I would have really liked marrying on the run, with tin cans dragging behind some Harley. Knowing me as she does, my mother probably wouldn't have been shocked anyway, so what would have been the point?

In mid-life, my notion of simple was more along the lines of my forebears: bride, groom, preacher, best man, maid of honor, corsage, kiss, dinner at some romantic little spot. Elaborate fairy-tale weddings seemed too *jeune fille* even when I was *jeune fille*, and it was frightful for me to imagine myself the center of a crowd's attention. Best of all, Simple would be less Special Event.

Darned if my notion of Simple didn't expand. It's a common bridal hazard, and apparently mid-lifers aren't immune. In my case, the reason was clear: I was proud of my impending marriage, and I suddenly realized I wanted to *share* it—not with the world, mind you, but with a few special people. Making phone calls and E-mails the next day wouldn't quite cut it.

Still, my wedding would be mature and understated, more in the manner of a second wedding. I would later realize my concept of second weddings was dated and narrow. One second-timer, who married before a Justice of the Peace the first time, pulled out all the stops 35 years later with a 16-piece orchestra, more than 4,000 roses and a beaded, designer gown. (If Barbra Streisand can't pull out all the stops, who among us can?)

Not counting money, fame, or power, Streisand is typical of the mid-life second-timer: She's been here, done this, and she's not likely to do it the same way again. Her tastes have changed. Her budget has changed, generally for the better. She's in charge this time. She's more in touch with her tolerance level for Wedding Hell. She's less anxious about what's "right." She'll invest more in quality than in quantity. *Let's get the good champagne* versus *Let's add another 50 people to the guest list.* And she won't stage a rerun of the wedding she had with the other guy.

So if your first wedding was a full-blown extravaganza, this time you may go for something small and restrained. If you married barefoot and tie-dyed before a swami in a daisy field, you may now go for rock-solid tradition—chapel, lace and "Here Comes the Bride." If you went down to City Hall without fanfare, you may want to be surrounded this time by everyone you know and love.

Only one rule applies: *There are no rules.*

"Up until recently, a second wedding was still viewed as an embarrassment," says John Ludlum, a stationer of 18 years. "You were supposed to do it quietly. Today, people who remarry are much more open about it."

And why not, in an age when some people have *divorce* parties? Still, if today's wedding etiquette books mention second weddings at all, they tend to do it at the very end and in a manner that seems deliberately hushed and tactful.

The first-time wedding in mid-life is so odd, no rules have ever existed. Hence there are none to break! Whether you choose to behave like an ingenue, a matron or a hybrid, no one can rightly tell you "That's just not done." You're a maverick. Enjoy the moment.

Regardless of size or style, first marriage or fourth, mid-life weddings seem to be more fun. According to various wedding consultants, mid-lifers focus more on partying and less on propriety, ritual, scripting and precision choreography. Moreover, the guests are generally confident, rightly or wrongly, that they're witnessing two mature people making a wise and wonderful move. However joyous the weddings of younger couples, the mood is often filtered through a layer of hope, as in: *I sure hope these young people know what they're doing.*

"I've decided I'm not going to any more weddings of children," said a fellow mid-life newlywed. "I'll go when they're old enough to figure things out."

For all these reasons, mid-life weddings are more at ease. That certainly seemed the case at a wedding reception I attended at age 13 for some friends of my parents. My memory of the details is shot, but I haven't forgotten the overall level of jubilation that filled a huge bright, ballroom. I suspect the couple's friends had been waiting for this moment for many years. The moment had arrived, and the atmosphere was euphoric.

No matter what kind of wedding you ultimately have, you're probably in for a good time.

On Matters of Style . . .
Consider This

• **Again, forget about rules.** Don't let anyone convince you that traditional weddings are inappropriate or silly for mature brides. Nor should you refrain from being as avant-garde as you please. Be guided by gut feeling and bank account.

• **If you're a second-timer, consider doing things differently than you did before.** Have the big wedding you didn't have. Or run like heck from the big wedding you *did* have.

• **If you're a first-timer, be as schizophrenic as you wanna be.** You can have a wedding that's youthful and giddy in some respects and mature and sophisticated in others.

• **Invest in quality rather than quantity.** Whatever your budget, steer it toward better food, champagne or photography. You can skip the balloon arches and other youthful props. Buy one over-the-top floral arrangement instead of wall-to-wall carnations. Order good stationery rather than excess pieces. Hire one top-notch violinist or guitarist in place of a five-piece band. A gourmet buffet is better—and more sociable—than sit-down rubber chicken.

• **Keep the script to a minimum.** Mid-lifers don't need to program the wedding to death. *At 4:17, the groom will dance with the mother of the bride.* Improvise and go with the flow.

• **Focus on fun rather than doing things "right."**

~

Downtown or Cow Town?: When and Where to Wed

"My fiancé wants to get married on a Monday," complained a young woman attending a bridal expo. "That's his day off."

Most couples are more mindful of the convenience of others. Sure, it's your day, but since you've asked another five or 500 people to make a special effort to share it with you, you'll try to plan it with the majority in mind. Scheduling a wedding on a weekend is one of those age-old traditions that's age-old for good reason.

Scheduling can be especially tough for mid-lifers. Given work schedules and personal obligations, it's tough enough finding a mutually ideal time for the bride and groom, let alone everyone else. The fact that we don't prepare for our weddings years in advance helps; we have a better feel for our calendars over shorter terms. And we'll usually make a date and stick with it, come hell or come boss. Several years ago, a young manager I know postponed her wedding date to tend to job demands. As of this writing, she has yet to reschedule. She has yet to realize the Real Stuff in Life. She also has yet to realize that business will prevail without her. No one is indispensable.

You may be familiar with the intrepid television network news correspondent who seems happiest in cross fire. Two days before her wedding, bomb blasts ripped open the U.S. embassies in Nairobi and Dar es Salaam. Did she rush to either scene? Nah. Nor did her groom, a spokesperson for the State Department. They wed *and* took their three-week honeymoon as planned.

Still, our timing can be impacted by circumstances of life, if not of work.

"I prefer spring," Future Husband told me. "Any date is fine with me. Pick any date at all."

"How about April 21?"

"No."

That was the date of his last wedding.

Elaine had to postpone her wedding date by three months. Some divorce papers didn't get signed as quickly as anticipated. Printed invitations hit the trash.

Jackie's beloved stepmother died a week before her wedding day. Postpone or not? Not. The wedding went on, though Jackie was not in optimal bridal spirits.

If planning a wedding incredibly bestows excess energy upon you, consider scheduling a wedding *weekend*.

Multiple-event weddings are a growing trend among couples of all ages. The day after her wedding, Gail held a barbecue at her brother's house for her out-of-town guests. Elaine's Saturday evening wedding was followed by a Sunday brunch. Both brides were able to spend more clear-headed time with their guests after an overnight descent from the bridal cloud. That's a big plus if some guests are special people you rarely see. Moreover, when travelers spend time and money just to be at your three-hour wedding, it's awfully nice to give them something extra. And if your wedding is in Dustbowl USA, what else are they going to find to do while waiting for the next train, plane or stagecoach outta there?

Now, *where* are you going to wed? Dustbowl, Metropolis, or Fantasy Island? That's often a bigger question than timing.

The bride's hometown is the traditional place. But you may have lived away from your hometown so long, you hardly remember the name of the street a block from where you lived. In fact, it's hardly the town you knew anyway. The five-and-ten is now a video rental place. The vegetable farm with the roadside stand is now a housing development. Your childhood friends are gone, and frankly most may be less important to you now than the friends you've made in later years. Even your parents may have left town. If they haven't, maybe they fully expect you to wed in your hometown church. And in the spirit of liberation: What about the convenience and sentiments of the *groom's* hometown friends and relations?

Most of your friends may live in the place where you live in now. Or they may have spread all over the planet. Or they may be concentrated in some other town where you lived for many years before relocating to the place where you live now. And even if the new place is really neat, it may lack emotional signficance for you. Besides, to put a wedding together, how do you begin to navigate an unfamiliar sea? Who are the good florists? Where can you get a decent buy on champagne? What pastor or house of worship is meaningful to you?

In the end, you'll probably choose a locale that offers at least a little sentiment along with convenience. But compromise may be in order.

Annette and Bob, both Americans, wed in Mexico, her beloved adopted country. Jeanne and her husband, also Americans, married in Myanmar. They weren't trying to be exotic. That's where they happened to relocate suddenly for his job. Yet you can always have your wedding someplace devoid of personal attachment just because it speaks to you.

For my location, one of those Wedding Elves pointed me in the direction of my island retreat of some 35 years—until I mentioned the idea to my friend Dolores:

"It takes so long to get there. The ferry reservations are so complicated. It's so hard to get plane reservations. Finding a place to stay is so confusing. It's so expensive," she whined. She was right. I was on the verge of subjecting friends and family to an odyssey that could make even a Monday wedding seem considerate. Furthermore, I learned that getting licensed in Massachusetts is a relatively unsimple process, involving medical consultations and waivers for out-of-state officiants.

So much for geography. What kind of *settings* do mid-lifers choose for their weddings?

For receptions, few of us book those one-stop-shopping catering factories offering rigid choices of menus, music and decor. There's nothing more impersonal than going to the ladies' room and finding a Twilight Zone of five other brides sharing "your" special day. Some of you may select a hotel or a restaurant with a private room. But as you've grown more sentimental with age, you may prefer your wedding venue to make a personal statement. It may be the botanical garden where you and your partner have spent many a romantic Sunday afternoon. It may be the restaurant where the two of you had your first date.

Maybe you'll have your wedding at home—yours, his or yours together. It's your nest, a cradle of your love. The decor already reflects you. And if it's a small gathering, you can use your own beloved china, crystal or linens that you may have collected over time, rather than compromising (and spending) on rented stuff.

Another Wedding Elf implored me to have the wedding at my childhood home. Both ceremony and reception would take place there—again, in the interest of Simple. No directions to print. No caravan to organize from one place to the next. No losing of guests en route.

My wedding would be in the house where, as a five-year-old peeking into freshly plastered rooms, I discovered that blue—blue!—porcelain fixtures had been installed in the new master bathroom. But my bathroom, I learned, would be common old white. I cried buckets. My mother tried to cheer me by changing the subject. Walking me down sawdusty stairs to the empty living room, she sang "Here comes the bride. . . ." I was having none of it. I kept bawling.

Forty years later, I still remembered that first walk down the stairs. *Here comes the bride. . . .*

On When and Where . . .
Consider This

• **Schedule far enough ahead to take care of business.** If you're a typical mid-lifer trying to fast-track your wedding timetable, calm down a bit. Before setting a date, allow ample time to prepare a prenup. Allow *more* than ample time if you have yet to finalize your divorce or his. Check the licensing process in the state where you'll wed. In some places, there may be a required waiting period or time-nibbling procedures.

• **Think people before place.** Nail down where you want to wed after generally deciding whom you'd like to invite as guests or members of the wedding party. Then pick a location that appeals to you *and* works for almost everyone else. After all, isn't "who" more important than "where"? If there's only one important person who may be inconvenienced, do what you can to help. Set a date that best fits his schedule, for example, or assume part of his travel expense.

• **Stick with the date you set.** Above all, don't let work or other mundane issues force a change in your plans. Consider letting the boss know of your wedding date well in advance, lest she schedule you to make a major presentation the day before. If possible, try to take some vacation time before and after the event.

• **Hire a consultant or enlist a knowledgeable committee if you wed in unfamiliar territory.** Otherwise, prepare to spend a whole lot of time doing your own research.

• **Go for a setting that "speaks" to you.** It may be a sentimental spot or simply a beautiful one. If you hold your ceremony or reception in a hotel ballroom or a plain-vanilla public room, make your personal statement with the decor.

Other Prenups: Showers, Parties, Luncheons, and Such

For many young brides, having a wedding means having a full wedding *season*. Between engagement day and wedding day, they may have months of parties, showers, receptions and whatnot.

Mid-life couples barely give themselves enough engagement time to schedule a wedding, let alone a wedding season. Enthusiastic friends and family members may want to do you the kindness of throwing you one type of party or another, and some mid-lifers eagerly embrace the hoopla. Most of you, however, will keep hoopla to a minimum. Some of it seems silly. Some of it seems superfluous. Some of it may seem terrific, but you haven't the time or energy for it. Don't feel obliged by tradition to do anything you don't want to do. Nor should you feel obliged, for fear of hurting anyone's feelings. A polite "no thank you" may be in order.

There's a potpourri of common ancillary events.

ENGAGEMENT PARTY?

Let's just call it a wedding reception and put a ceremony in front of it.

BRIDESMAIDS' LUNCHEON/TEA?

Mid-life brides often choose not to have bridesmaids in the first place. If you do, and if they're truly maids, they're children. If they're your peers, for goodness' sake, call them something else! In any event, you probably won't have more than a couple of "attendants," and chances are slim these days that all of you live in close proximity. Still, if possible, taking your attendants to lunch or buying them small gifts is certainly a nice gesture in return for their support. Unlike the young bride with eight ladies-in-waiting, you can plan a luncheon—at home or at a restaurant—that's as impromptu and relaxed as any other lunch date with a pal or two.

SHOWER?

Now we're talking.

Showers know no age or generation. For years, long before I was comfortable with the idea of ever marrying, I coveted the bridal shower. I even hosted a few. Few experiences are as uplifting as the warmth and hilarity of the company of the sisterhood.

Friends should forget about the "surprise" shower, unless they know the bride well enough to know she'd love it. For many mid-lifers, life is unnerving enough as it is.

For brides of any age, showers generally combine good food and great conversation. Without shame, we may indulge in "feminine" food like salade niçoise or finger sandwiches—maybe followed by chocolate cheesecake. We may drink tea or punch out of dainty cups. The punch may have Punch. And—believe it, guys—we discuss subjects other than men.

What mid-life showers leave *out* of the usual picture are indignities like wearing paper-plate hats decorated with ribbons or pleated skirts made from gift wrap. Nor are we and our guests forced into silly games, like getting clothes-pinned for crossing one's legs the wrong way. Of course, there's nothing wrong with reviving a younger, sillier time if you and your friends feel like it.

Gifts supposedly are the point of a shower. I think it's just the excuse—but not a bad one. The kitchen theme pretty much died long ago, when liberated women refused to reinforce the idea that kitchen chores are women's work. Moreover, most of today's brides and grooms have lived on their own at least briefly, so they've already got the basics. In fact, they've got two of each. But if cooking is your hobby, getting showered with gourmet gadgets is great.

Lingerie has always been my favorite theme. As young singles, we often reserve our few pieces of "the good stuff" for special occasions. Later, as we grow in self-esteem, we realize that *every* day is a special occasion, and we want to celebrate ourselves right down to the skin. So what if no one else is the wiser? And so what if our bodies' best days in lingerie are flying by? Our stage is the boudoir, not the Victoria's Secret catalog.

Brides traditionally make their own guest lists, usually opting for either a multigenerational shower or a gang of peers. The former may be more formal; the latter, more laid back. But as women approach mid-life, the distinction becomes more blurred. Your peers cover a wider age span now. Among elders and juniors alike, you've become less guarded. Your sister, ten years younger, is no longer the "kid" sister. She may have a husband, children, a Ph.D. and the first signs of cellulite. Likewise, the co-worker ten years your senior, with grand-children, is one of your cronies, too.

I had two showers. I hardly deserved two, but I accepted both invitations gladly.

For the first, I'd just about completed my guest list—of peers, in this case—when I foolishly peeked into an etiquette book. The author insisted that shower guests *must* be wedding guests, too. This law could be waived only if the shower was hosted by a distinct group, such as the church choir or your fellow nurses from the surgical ward. Uh-oh.

Most of the women on my list were not invited to the wedding. They were local friends of loose connection or no connection at all. Hence, Ms. Etiquette would hardly qualify People-I-Know-and-Like as a "distinct group." I was trampling the law! I panicked and consulted one of the shower hostesses.

"It's okay, since the wedding is out of town," she concluded. Oh, all right. But still, just because she and I thought that a reasonable exemption, what if some of the guests didn't? For all their modern attitudes, what if they were traditionalists at the core, deeply offended by my discourtesy? Did I need to make a speech at the shower—*It's like this, see, I'm planning just a small and simple wedding . . . ?* Momentarily, like any young bride, I worried about what was "right."

Then I put everyone I wanted on the guest list. The more we move about during our lives, gathering new friends in new venues, it seems entirely right to celebrate our marriages with different events for different people in different places.

Shower number 2 was at the invitation of my mother's reading club, an honestly distinct group of women with whom she's gathered every other Tuesday evening since I was in junior high school. One member is the mother of my childhood best friend. Another is the mother of children I molded into heads of families and professional practices. (Okay, so I was the baby-sitter.) The few members I don't know well, I *feel* I know well; my mother's sprinkled her conversations with their names for 10, 20, 30 years or more. They, in turn, know my every educational, occupational and geographic move. This shower was somewhat more poised than the peer shower, but it was much more grounded in sentiment. I was wrapped comfortably in the wings of all my "mothers." By the way, some of these mothers had some pretty hot ideas about lingerie.

Nowadays, many liberated brides and grooms have coed showers. It's kind of an engagement party with gifts. The theme might be wine, for example, or something else both you and your groom appreciate.

Bear in mind that invited guests who have conflicts on the date of a given event may want to treat you to lunch, dinner, cocktails, or whatever at another time. One event often breeds a few more.

REHEARSAL DINNER?

Let's step back: *Rehearsal?* Is our ceremony some stage play? And why do a ceremony twice? We might as well call the rehearsal the wedding, sign some papers, and make it official. For complex ceremonies with numerous players, rehearsals are overwhelmingly advisable. But once my pastor agreed we hardly needed a rehearsal for our simple ritual with a cast of three, that nailed it for me. Affirmation from the event's spiritual authority was all I needed.

Dinner was another matter. I wholeheartedly embraced the idea of a get-together in advance of the next day's formalities. This would involve the full wedding "party"—me, Future Husband, and Heather, my goddaughter and bridesmaid—as well as members of the respective families, ranging in age from eight to seventy-eight. I wanted to create bonding time, and food is generally a good ice breaker. Granted, no two strangers have ever bonded in two hours, but it would be a start.

"Are we going to a fancy French restaurant?" Heather asked hopefully. Heather is the unlikely product of two Californians whose idea of getting dressed up is to put on the least worn pair of jeans.

No, Heather, the dinner would be *casual*. Extremely non-Special Event. Relaxed. Shorts, sneakers, whatever. I'm not through with my rebellion, either.

Traditionally, the rehearsal dinner is the groom's parents' moment in the sun—and in the purse. As noted, mid-lifers have often been down the aisle before. His parents may have already done the rehearsal-dinner thing. The idea may not be fresh or exciting anymore. If they want to host yet another rehearsal dinner, fine. If you or someone else wants to do it, that's fine, too. As with the wedding, the question of who contributes the effort or expense is totally flexible.

For roughly 14 people, we reserved nearly half the dining room at a small, comfy Italian place. Future Husband picked up the tab.

I'd spent half the day picking up in-laws from airports and half the evening looking for the restaurant. The organized bride would have tried to have everyone fly in to the *same* airport, or she would have asked a friend to make at least one pickup. She would also have made a trial run to the restaurant days before. But heavens, all that would have been too Special Event. At dinner, I felt too good to notice I was bone-tired. Bridal fever was beginning to take hold. Once full of pasta, however, I canceled the rest of the evening's agenda: fireworks at the nearby amusement park, a sentimental childhood hangout. I believe everyone else over 40 was equally relieved.

BACHELOR PARTY?

The bride's version debuted as the "bachelorette" party when it was pioneered, I believe, by my newly liberated generation years ago. The motivation: Why should men have all the fun? They're hardly the only ones losing their independence.

The traditional point of the bachelor party is to celebrate the high times you supposedly can't have once you're married. Yet chances are, you're going to keep doing most of what you like after marriage, with your husband or without. Maybe you've been living with him for a considerable time, which means you have little or no secret wild life in the first place. And if you're a mid-lifer, what is this "wild" life anyway? A rented video and a pint of Cherry Garcia?

Therefore, you may forgo this last hurrah. Then again, you may look at it as another excuse, if you need one, to celebrate your transition.

In the early days, many women's bachelor parties aimed to copy men's bachelor parties, with elements such as abundant booze, ribald humor, and strippers. But as time went by, women began fashioning their parties in their own spirit. For many, that spirit rules out neither booze nor strippers. But for others—mid-lifers in particular—the bachelor party has evolved into something more imaginative. One woman flew to New Orleans with a few pals for a prewedding weekend of revelry in the French Quarter. Another woman scheduled an afternoon with her buddies at a spa, getting relaxed and pampered. The most titillating feature was the muscular masseur, whose physical interest in women apparently was strictly professional.

On a more down-to-earth level, you can go for a country drive and a picnic. You can kick back at a friend's place with a pizza. (Don't make the delivery guy strip.) Or you can take this opportunity to reprise a livelier past—by going to a disco, for example. You can even go *way* back, with a record player and some dusty 45s.

There's no law that says a bachelor party must happen the night before the wedding. Mid-lifers in particular should strongly consider a break with this tradition. At the very least, don't party until the wee hours. You know full well your energy and looks don't recover as quickly as they used to.

On Showers, etc. . . .
Consider This

• **Say "no" kindly to anyone who offers an engagement party or shower you don't want.**

• **Speak up in advance about gifts.** Even if you're not the hostess, you have a right to dictate gift policy. Keep gift-giving affairs to a minimum, or limit some affairs to inexpensive novelties.

• **Consider prenuptial events as ways to extend the celebration geographically.** You can thereby be more inclusive of people in various places—your town, his town, your or his hometown, or other town.

• **Don't bite off more events than you can chew.** Even if you're the pampered guest rather than the hostess, a jammed schedule can make you weary.

• **Definitely don't bite off too much during the final week.** Avoid clogging your calendar just before the Big Mo. You'll have enough to do with last-minute wedding preparations. If you expect any time left over at all, reserve it for relaxation.

The Posse: Help on Your Own Terms

Yes, it's "your" wedding, but no woman is an island. And as full and busy as your life is already, that's mainly a good thing.

MOM AND DAD

"How are you enjoying your honeymoon?" I asked a young newly-wed in Key West.

"It's great," she said. "I'm so glad to get away from my *family*." I'm optimistic that she was also glad to be with her husband, celebrating the start of a new life. But that wasn't her top-of-mind thought.

Mid-life couples, too, encounter family, but we've got control on our side. Conspicuously absent from the captain's bridge is Mom. Hallelujah! This bonus belongs somewhere in the top-ten list of reasons to get married later rather than sooner. Long ago, you laid down the *burden* of Mom, and vice versa. Over time, the two of you have mellowed into partners and friends—fellow members of the universal sisterhood, dues and all. Mom won't dictate the wedding agenda, and you won't pout or shout. You'll listen to her ideas. You'll even *ask* for her ideas. In the end, the day is yours.

"I don't want to wear a chastity veil," sighed a young bride-to-be and co-worker, "but my fiancé's mother insists."

Your *fiancé's* mother?

Wedding consultant Sylvia Garcia agrees that Mom's absence from the throne is helpful: "Mom's input isn't necessarily a bad thing. But she's one more person adding a point of view, and that slows down the decision-making process."

Mom dethroned may still contribute valuable time and effort to the wedding's execution—if she feels like it. In my case, I beseeched Mom. She resided in the wedding location, and I didn't.

"I'll pay for the wedding if you'll put it together," I suggested.

"I was going to say the same thing to you," she replied.

Mom was retired; I was consumed. We were each in a life phase that did not move either of us to take on the task, however merry the purpose. Your mother may have an additional reason to shun wedding work. For you or your siblings, perhaps she's done this a few times before.

Mom and I ended up a team, sharing—with Future Husband—both work and expense.

As for fathers, they generally still bankroll the weddings of young daughters. Dad doesn't otherwise "do" the wedding, but he holds status as executive producer nonetheless. Though he may choose to hand over the credit cards to the women and then stay out of the way, he may weigh in occasionally on matters of extravagance, pro or con. I used to joke when I was younger that if I ever had a wedding, I'd stay home and watch it on television. My father, left unbridled, would have mounted the extravaganza of all time, perhaps at the Taj Mahal.

Mid-life couples, as well as some younger ones these days, pay for their own weddings. That's all the more reason the day belongs to you and you alone. To some fathers, that may be a relief. But other fathers may feel displaced, especially if the wedding is your first. It occurred to me that maybe there was a dusty bank account somewhere in the name of "Shelley's Wedding," opened by my father the day I was born.

Imagine the earned interest. Parkinson's disease had since reduced my father's communications to fluttering eyelids and silently moving lips. If it could have brought back Dad's health and laughter, I would have eagerly done the Taj Mahal, televised and all.

That's the potential downside of marrying older. When Elaine married at 19, her mother orchestrated everything. By the time she remarried some 30 years later, Mom had retired to that great reception in the sky. Elaine hardly found comfort in having Mom out of the picture. Annette's and Bob's parents were gone, too, but remembered in the words of the pastor. If we have parents who are alive and healthy when we marry, we're lucky, and we know it.

THE COMMITTEE

After my buddy Donna got engaged many years back, she summoned a bunch of us to her apartment one afternoon to brainstorm ideas for the big event. It was a girl thing; the groom-to-be had nothing to do with it. In those days, no one would have expected him to get involved. Most of the participants were full of suggestions: *When I got married, we did this-and-that.* Or *At my cousin's wedding, blah-blah-blah.* I, on the other hand, had little to contribute. Aside from having no experience at the altar, I had little experience among the Dearly Beloved. Huge as my extended family is, weddings are rare and often spontaneous. Weddings among my friends have been rare, too. I was a flower girl twice, a bridesmaid once. I paid little attention to the details.

Mid-lifers, too, can enlist committees. Unlike Donna, you'll probably conceive your ideas independently, but some of the execution can be delegated to friends and family members. Of course, organizing a wedding, let alone a committee meeting, is trouble enough. Convening even a small committee may be impractical. Over the years, your would-be committee members—close friends and family members— may have spread across the country and beyond. But that's okay, in this age of E-mail, faxes, and overnight mail. Keep the number of members to a minimum—maybe even to one. And just as at work, meet only if necessary.

Your ad hoc committee members are busy people, too, and your wedding is not their top priority. Therefore, the tasks you delegate ought to be limited in scope and, if at all possible, of interest to the doer. Ask the photography buff to check out photographers, for example. Ask the gourmet cook to review the caterers. Ask the avid gardener to recommend flower arrangements. Ask the music teacher to scout musicians. Most of all, you need members who don't require much supervision. That would defeat the point. Elaine, who mainly inhabits airplanes and airports, enlisted a friend as her amateur planner on the home front. The friend misunderstood "harpist" and scouted—successfully!—a harmonica player instead.

"You're the emcee," Annette informed her sister—moments before the ceremony. I, too, forgot to enlist Big Mo support until reality loomed large. The ceremony would be, you know, Simple. It was scripted down to the minute. The wedding party was minuscule. Yet it finally dawned on me a week before the wedding that I couldn't direct even this basic a ceremony and be in it, too. Somebody else would have to whisper "go" to the right people at the right times.

"Donna? I have a favor to ask of you."

Donna was the perfect choice of wedding director. In the '70's, whenever I gave a party, it was Donna who would run around my apartment making sure no brassieres were hanging from doorknobs. It was Donna who'd whisper "You're running out of ice." Donna was and is the consummate worrywart—a functional, problem-solving worrywart, thank goodness. And now, instead of sitting in the congregation worrying if everything was okay behind the scenes, she could *be* behind the scenes, worrying firsthand and doing something about it. I merely insisted that as soon as it was my turn to emerge, she be seated among the rest of my Dearly Beloved.

THE PRO

You can hire a professional wedding consultant, if your budget allows. For me, that seemed over-the-top at the time. Too Charles-and-Di. Too Special Event. Yet if Greta, my most annoyingly organized friend, hired a wedding consultant, who was I to think I could do without?

Prior to selecting a consultant, be sure to meet the candidates personally, no matter how well they've been recommended. For mid-lifers in particular, rapport is critical. Many wedding consultants are accustomed to working mainly with younger brides. You need a consultant not *in loco parentis*, but rather *in loco* partner. A mature young consultant may be fine, so long as you're mature enough to accept his or her maturity. But your ideal consultant may be of your own generation and gender—someone who can identify.

If you're short on both time and ideas, you can have a consultant do it all. *I wear a size 6; just tell me when and where to show up.* At the other extreme, you can limit the consultant's involvement to specific, well-defined tasks. *Book Country Caterers; order the scampi.* Or you can hire a professional to serve simply as director on the wedding day, leaving you to focus on higher spiritual matters than place cards.

As one consultant attests, last-minute mid-lifers aren't the easiest customers. "Ten minutes before one ceremony, when I could have been doing a hundred other things, I'm running back and forth between dressing rooms, getting the bride's and groom's signatures on the prenup."

THE SECRETARY

A good and less costly alternative to the wedding professional is a temporary secretary, who can manage invitations, run errands, send the down payment to the florist and so on. You can hire through an agency or recruit a freelancer.

If you have a secretary at work, and if he's a masochist, he may be available for moonlighting. No one knows your habits and hot buttons better than the secretary who's worked with you for a considerable time. We're talking *paid* moonlighting—don't expect the secretary to do more than the rarest favor for free. It's neither right nor reliable. Nor should you ask the secretary to perform wedding tasks on his day job, unless you happen to own the business. Know this: Nosy coworkers will hang the secretary by his thumbs, if need be, for the latest update on your event, mishaps and all.

FUTURE HUSBAND

I've saved the best for last. For mid-lifers in particular, the wedding isn't a "bridal" event; it's a bride-and-groom event. You and your partner are the ultimate committee. You're costars and coproducers with equal billing. Every wedding decision is a consensus. A preview of the rest of your life, isn't it? Like you, fortunately, your partner probably doesn't have the patience to argue the small stuff.

Is it okay with you if we don't have a receiving line?

Fine.

Perhaps the biggest and best difference between the young and the mid-life groom is that the mid-life groom is sincerely interested in the wedding plans. He may fuss over vows, menus and the guest list. Check out a bridal registry or a stationer's shop: Young brides are there with their mothers; mid-life brides are there with their grooms. Some of these guys get downright obsessed with choices of teacups and such. If their golf buddies could see them now. . . .

The tasks for my wedding ended up being split ad hoc among Mom, Future Husband and myself. Whoever thought of it, generally did it. Whoever did it, generally paid for it. Each of us wanted to do more, not less. The bonus was witnessing the blossoming of a bond between Future Husband and Mom. It continues today.

On Getting Help . . .
Consider This

• **Don't shun help with ideas or execution.** But be selective about what you want help with and by whom.

• **Don't overstaff.** Otherwise, the work of coordination will exceed the work itself.

• **Try to assign family members or friends to tasks that are likely to interest them.** But if you need to assign some drudgery, such as stuffing invitations, turn it into a party, with food and drink. Don't pull a Tom Sawyer; share the drudgery with the team.

• **Avoid recruiting volunteers at the last minute.** Think and ask ahead.

• **Don't leave out Future Husband.** He probably wants to be involved. If not, work him anyway. If he's not the flower or *canapé* type, ask him to coordinate something less dainty: liquor, transportation or reception music.

Solomonic Proportions: The Guest List

"How many invitations did you order?"

Nice try, Mom. I've set my guest limit at 37. It would be bigger than the preacher-plus-two-witness wedding I first envisioned but small enough to be semi-intimate. I wouldn't have to walk down the aisle under the gaze of a thousand eyes. I'd have time to chat with everyone there. The next day, I'd *remember* who was there. I was also under the false impression that small naturally means Simple. I know better now.

"I planned to have 30-something people, too," said my coworker Lisa. "I ended up with 200."

Yikes. Apparently there'd been a plea to invite the groom's godmother. Who turned out to be an aunt. One of several. Most of whom came attached to husbands and children. Which meant having to invite the *bride's* aunts . . . and so on.

This bride was just young and under too many thumbs, I concluded. All I had to do was take a tally of close friends and family and call it a day. It's a simple plan in principle if not in practice. Several objectives can go into the making of a guest list. They boil down to inviting people you love, inviting people you like and inviting people it would be difficult for any number of reasons not to invite. The longer you've been on Earth, the more of all these people you know. If you're trying to keep things small, you've got some Solomonic decisions to make and, regrettably, maybe some feelings to hurt. But, as my coworker learned the hard way, it takes only one person to open the floodgates.

"It's so hard trying to explain to people that we want to keep things small," fretted Gina, a second-timer who did the big wedding the first time around.

I've heard of people inviting the multitudes in the hope that some will decline. It may sound like a tactic of the young and immature, but in truth it's often their parents who are behind it. Insincerity is just plain wrong in my ad hoc book of etiquette. Plus it can backfire—*oh, no, Helen and the kids are coming*—and you'll deserve it. Better to remember that being politic cuts two ways: If you feel inviting Cousin A means having to invite Cousins B, C and D, you can invite all four *or* none of the above.

The institution of family, and the expansion thereof, is what marriage is about. Most couples therefore want family among the celebrants. Families, however, are pyramid schemes. If you're a mid-lifer, your four grandparents may be gone. Even your parents may be gone. But over time, you or your siblings have brought forth children and maybe grandchildren; your cousins have begotten more cousins. If you're having a large wedding, that's fine. If you're having a family reunion, that's fabulous. But for the small wedding, a large extended family spells peril.

Families are fraught with sensitivity. In my case, furthermore, I was the only daughter of lavish Brother/Uncle/Cousin Marcus. To some family members, I suspect my wedding was supposed to be the all-time extravaganza, not to be missed. Marcus, however, was not in charge.

Work experience has taught me that decisions go down easier with the troops when they follow policy—even bad policy—rather than some knee-jerk whim of the boss. Hence, I set policy: From each side of my family, we would invite just one aunt or uncle plus spouse. I bent the rule only for Cousin Bonnie and her family, who satisfied my Lives Nearby clause.

My mother panicked. "Some people are going to be upset," she said.

I know. I can handle it.

"They're going to be upset with *me*."

Even when you're in charge of your wedding, some traditionalists will still attribute all that's right or wrong with it to Mom. But had anyone questioned the guest list out loud, I had answers at the ready.

Why did you invite Ted and Joan but not Tim and Charlene?

See Section H, Paragraph III.

For divorced brides or grooms, whose families may still feel bitter or awkward, the guest list can create considerable anxiety. Should you invite your ex-sister-in-law who's still your good friend? What about your ex-husband's friends who became your friends, too? Will they be embarrassed if you invite them? Will they feel offended if you don't? You may have to choose between putting pressure on yourself and putting pressure on them.

Children—yours or his, young or old—are the most sensitive consideration. On Future Husband's side of the family, the two most coveted invitees were his sons. Had they healed sufficiently from their parents' divorce? Had they accepted us as a couple, let alone as husband and wife? Without hesitation, the elder—who'd rather be shot than leave Texas for a trip to New York—said yes. The younger, who would have to make a whirlwind overseas trip, said yes, too.

"Of course I'm coming. You're my father, aren't you?" I can see Future Husband's eyes brimming now.

Similarly, two of Bob's three sons traveled to witness the blessing of his marriage to Annette. Elaine's partner, on the other hand, had no such luck with his invitation to his daughter. Perhaps the wedding was too soon on the heels of divorce. And perhaps a daughter can identify more closely with a mother's pain. In any case, neither the bride nor the groom had a single relative at their wedding for various reasons—serious illness, travel expense, death, and estrangement (or at least attitude). The couple was happy to be surrounded by loving friends, but at moments, the disappointment was apparent.

Estrangement is real and painful in many families. No bride or groom should feel pressured to invite anyone who evokes bitter feelings. It makes no difference if others feel those feelings are unwarranted, fixable or worthy of putting on the back burner for a day. Nothing and no one should tighten the jaws of either the bride or the groom on this occasion. Nothing should taint their experience of harmony and bliss— even if someone else is wounded.

It was important to me, if less so to Future Husband, that we strive for a little balance between his friends and family and mine. We didn't expect 50–50, given his distant homeland. Yet I didn't want him to feel overwhelmed by strangers. One guest made the list for knowing us both before we knew each other. Future Brother-in-Law and his family crossed the waters to share our moment. Limiting my side of the guest list to close friends and family also helped; by now, most were friends or acquaintances of his, too. This strategy aided my implementation of The Policy: I invited the aunt and the uncle that Future Husband already knew.

For mid-lifers who've been together for, say, a decade or more, friends often overlap entirely. The two families also may know each other well. Hence, the relaxed gaiety at the mid-life wedding of my parents' friends years ago. There's less tension among the crowd. Less scrutiny of the "other side." Less dread of the same in return.

Unlike me, you may want to include one and all in the celebration—all the childhood chums, the sorority sisters, the football teammates, the Chicago friends, the San Diego friends, the Baltimore friends, the friends from jobs 1, 2 and 3 and every last relative. Yet maybe you don't want the multitudes encroaching on the solemn intimacy of your ceremony. That's why a growing number of mid-lifers opt for two-part weddings.

With the two-parter, you can limit your ceremony to a handful of your closest loved ones, then have a blowout of a reception with everyone from your high school principal to the paper boy. You can even have the reception in a different town at a later date. "Like maybe *two months* later," suggested bride-to-be Gina. The two-parter can also be an excellent compromise for any time-and-place dilemma. A few weeks after their ceremony in Mexico, Annette and Bob celebrated with folks back home in Texas. Maybe best of all, the two-parter relieves you of worrying about the caterer in the midst of reciting your vows.

The mid-life guest list is about *your* friends, not your parents' friends. Yet by now, you probably count some of your parents' friends—and friends' parents—as friends of your own. Now that you're all grownups, generational borders have relaxed. Mrs. Johnson may now be "Julia." One of my mother's friends recently gave me a humorous book on menopause, a gift I'd more likely expect from my menopausal peers. We've known some of these elders for years, if not forever. "I knew you before you were born," one family friend used to tell me. We've come to love them for supporting or at least witnessing our growth. Now we may want them to witness our latest big step.

When I was in kindergarten, another family friend used to escort me, along with his own daughter, to school every day on the subway. Forty years later, I asked him to serve as my wedding toastmaster—a role he fulfilled with characteristic wit and charm. Two years after that, he passed away. I cherish the special recent event by which I can always remember him. After all, the subway memories have grown quite fuzzy.

You can and should exclude from the guest list your father's loan officer, your mother's prospective client or any other parental associates you barely know or care about. Fortunately, parents of most mid-lifers won't propose such guests in the first place. But likewise, don't fall into the same trap with your own "important contacts" that you've developed over the years. A wedding shouldn't be confused with business entertainment (though a tax deduction is a compelling thought). Refrain from inviting anyone other than people you truly enjoy for the heck of it. Otherwise, you may be preoccupied with being "on" rather than having a spiritual moment or a rollicking good time. However, it's certainly fine to invite a boss or customer who's evolved into a true pal over the years.

We ended up inviting 50 people, and Mom's not to blame. Honestly, though, Future Husband and I never let the list get out of control. Fifty proved a fine limit: enough to feel like a party but not enough to feel like a circus. Some whose company we would have enjoyed were excluded, but no one who was there was unwanted. As of this writing, none of the excluded have ever complained or audibly sighed. I suspect most really didn't mind. Still, I'll always wonder about the feelings of a few.

On the Guest List . . . Consider This

• **If you're going for small, dare to be hard-hearted.** If hurting feelings is going to be more stressful to you than a bigger wedding, you may need to reconsider the size.

• **Never forget: It only takes one person to open the floodgates.**

• **Be evenhanded.** Politics cuts two ways. If you can't comfortably invite one coworker or club member without inviting them all, make a choice: all or none.

• **Do *not* put anyone on the invitation list whom you hope will not come.**

• **Take the heat.** If anyone puts Mom's feet to the fire about your guest list, step in and let that person know you're responsible.

• **Have a policy in your back pocket.** If anyone wants an explanation of why someone's excluded, you'll have a well-reasoned answer at the ready.

• **Don't submit to any pressure to invite an estranged family member or friend.** Nothing and no one should compromise your happiness on your wedding day.

• **Don't exclude someone you really want to invite.** Forget about issues like (a) she's associated with your previous marriage; (b) he probably won't come due to distance or

expense; (c) she's estranged from another guest; (d) he's probably still hurting from his divorce. These people will appreciate
knowing you want them there. Let them figure out what to do
on their own. Talking to them, in addition to sending a written
invitation, will help alleviate sensitivity.

• **To the extent possible, strive for balance between the
groom's friends and your own.**

• **By all means include the "grownups"—your parents'
friends—who over the years have become your friends,
too.**

• **Don't invite "contacts."** Your wedding is not business entertainment. Invite only business associates who happen to be
friends, too. Keep your wedding personal and fun.

Bridesmaids Don't Have Hot Flashes: The Wedding Party

C ousin Harold's wedding program reads like the credits for a movie. In addition to the standard wedding party members, the roster includes ushers, junior ushers, hostesses, bride's assistants—not to be confused with the bridesmaids—and a director. The wedding was held in the mutual hometown of the bride and groom, who apparently made a concerted effort to ensure everyone in town had a role and a title. That's kind of sweet. In retrospect, I could have used a director and maybe a bride's assistant myself.

A wedding party is a microcosm of the guest list—the chosen among the chosen. Hats off to the young bride who knows the wisdom of choosing sisters as bridesmaids rather than expanding the selection pool to that nebulous and political category of "friends." Of course, there's another type of young bride who chooses a number before choosing people. *Kathy had seven bridesmaids, so I think I'll have seven, too.* Then she has to fill the slots: three really good friends, the home girl she's barely talked to since high school, the annoying teenage niece, the groom's sister and . . . whomever.

As a mid-lifer, you're less likely to have friends who'll pout if they're not in your wedding's inner circle. Being there is important to them, but being in the "show" is not. Oversensitive people come in every age category, however. If your wedding party is small, that will help mollify the excluded. It's not like being left off a "short list" of 25 people.

It's a rare mid-lifer who wants a major wedding retinue in the first place. You may want a grand event, but not a fairy tale with a full cast of ladies-in-waiting, sergeants-at-arms, footmen, and what have you. You're becoming wife and husband, not queen and king. And you probably don't want to dress and coordinate that many people. Absent, for example, are the ushers who roll out that cloth the bride walks on— whatever it's called—lest she mess up her train—the train *you* probably will not wear. (See the chapter "No Nosegays.")

But I did want an usher to escort my parents into the ceremony. After all, they were the most honored of guests, as Future Husband's would have been, had they been there. My parents' godson was a smooth candidate for escort as well as a sentimental one. I congratulate myself for steering his stroller into a ditch some 30 years ago to save him from a speeding school bus.

To my surprise, Future Husband didn't want a best man. I always liked the idea of a man having his truest friend at his side on his most important occasion. Then again, at his age, he didn't need anyone holding him up. He was utterly confident. I, however, wanted a companion down the aisle. A sister in my corner. Choosing a close friend my own age would have been fine, though I wouldn't have known what to call her. "Bridesmaid" is ridiculous. "Bride's matron" seems, well, matronly. "Attendant" suggests the rest room.

Tess cleverly ditched labels altogether. "My sister's standing up for me," she explained.

Nowadays, the occasional bride will have a man stand up for her; the groom might have a woman.

I knew from the start that I wanted Heather standing up for me. A wedding is like Christmas in a way—an occasion made merrier by the presence of youth. And when the bride can no longer pass for youth, it's nice to freshen up the scene with someone who's still got it. Barbra

Streisand did it with an adorable bevy of goddaughters and stepdaughters. They did not detract from the bride's own glow.

Even for level-headed mid-lifers, a wedding is about dreams, wonder, and boundless faith. It's an afternoon's suspension of the real business of marriage, sweet and sour. Who as my companion could exude those ideals best? A friend who's been married nearly 20 years? A friend who recently divorced? A friend—take your pick—who's had no significant other for a decade or more? Sure, they've all still got romance in their blood. But not half as much as a 13-year-old girl.

"You only want *me*?" Heather asked.

"Only you."

"Not even my mother?"

"Nope."

Giggles. And with total justification and comfort, I could call her a bridesmaid. Many mid-lifers instill youth into the wedding party with their own flesh-and-blood children. Of course, children should never be pressured to participate. On the other hand, it shouldn't be assumed that a child doesn't want to. Many a child takes great delight in the wedding of a parent. Perhaps Mom's or Dad's happiness is contagious. Perhaps a wedding fulfills the child's dreams of a complete family. Whatever the reason, a child is often quite proud to serve as best man, flower girl, or any other capacity at Mom's or Dad's side. Lily, age 8, was exuberant not only as her mother's attendant but also as a self-appointed hostess, introducing guests to her new brothers and assertively pushing the guest book.

Future Husband was overjoyed simply to have his sons present. He asked no more of them.

Heather served a bonus purpose: Entering the spotlight behind her skirttails, I was spared being the only person to come down the aisle through the crowd. It's the rare mid-life bride who arrives at the altar on her father's arm—or on the arms of both parents, in the case of the Jewish bride. To be "given away" is antiquated enough for a bride in her twenties, to say nothing of a bride who's been out of the house for a quarter-century. And if you've been given away in marriage before, isn't it impossible to be given away again?

On their second trip down the aisle together, one father whispered to his daughter: "This is the last time I'm doing this." It was a prophetic statement. By her third marriage—the one that "took"—he was no longer alive.

As already mentioned, it's not unusual for mid-lifers to have at least one deceased parent. Others, like me, may have a parent who's severely ill or incapacitated. As our parents become creaky of limb, we treasure the time we have left with them all the more. What would I have done if my father were walking, talking, and eager to take me down the aisle? To heck with what's antiquated—I would have let him do so. No, I would have *invited* him to do so. Most fathers dream of this moment from the day we spring from the womb. If you're a first-timer, consider giving him this wedding gift. You can rightfully call the ritual "escorting" instead of "giving away."

On the Wedding . . . Consider This

• **Forgo the cast of thousands.** You're not staging a coronation, so keep the retinue simple. Don't feel obliged to give every family member or close friend a role. You can forgo excessive assignments such as Lighter of Candles or Carrier of Small Pillow with Fake Rings on It.

• **Instill youth.** It's nice to include young people in the wedding party. Granted, you and your groom will feel entirely young yourselves on that day. Adding the truly young will reinforce the mood.

• **Reserve the term "bridesmaid" for the young.** In fact, maybe the term is too antiquated to stick on anyone. By all means, have a favorite person by your side, regardless of age— or even gender. But if she has hot flashes, she is not a bridesmaid. Call her something else.

- **Inviting Dad to *escort* you is okay.** You're not being "given away." Nonetheless, it's fine to invite your father to escort you down the aisle, especially if it's your first time and his. It's also fine to walk down the aisle solo.

~

Be There or Be Square:
Invitations and Other Paper

Future Husband and I are at the shop of a venerable stationer in the nation's capital, where samples of past work read like:

The presence of your company is respectfully requested at a reception in honor of the Crown Prince of . . .

or

The Honorable and Mrs. High-Profile Senator cordially invite you to the wedding of their daughter Felicity Prudence. . . .

What better place to order invitations befitting the high quality we expected of every aspect of our wedding? Let me be clear: My concept of Simple wedding didn't mean chips and beer. It meant simply *elegant*, without extraneous detail (or work).

I could have shopped for a stationer the way I typically shop for a coat, checking half a dozen stores for the best quality at the deepest discount. But when the tonnage of vendors in the Yellow Pages made my eyes glaze over, I just zoomed in on a couple of tony-but-not-phony ads and headed to the shop closest to me. Our fellow customers included a 20-something bride with her mother and a 30-something bride with her groom. 'Nuff said. Like us, they were preparing for May weddings. Apparently I was on schedule or at least with the pack. I congratulated myself.

Many mid-lifers, especially the second-timers, go for nontraditional invitations. Whether custom-designed or off the shelf, their invitations make personal statements. They don't necessarily sport the "right" watermark, real engraving, unreadable typeface, flowery language, multiple enclosures and tissue inserts. They don't boast *See, we know the rules*.

Fortunately, Y2K closes the era of that ultimate excess: *In the year of our Lord One Thousand Nine Hundred. . . .*

More stationers today are specializing in the design of offbeat invitations. Some invitations nearly shout *Hey, it's a party, not a state funeral*. They may look as glittery as an invitation to a New Year's ball. Confetti may pour out of the envelope. The wording is casual: *Vicki and Bob are getting hitched!* Other invitations are softer and more sentimental—perhaps on rough parchment with pressed ferns. *After 14 years of spiritual affinity, Janet and Doug will seal their bonds of love. . . .* Flower children never die. They just put on shoes.

Leave it to me to be difficult. I wanted a traditional *and* personal invitation. As a first-timer, I wanted an element of formality. As a child of the '60's, I also wanted free expression. But I am not at an avant-garde stationer. I am at this crusty shop in Washington, a town where conformity rules. Maybe it's a Southern thing.

"You cannot write a personal note inside a formal invitation," the salesperson advised me.

Hey, I'm not some fall-in-with-the-troops Washingtonian. I can do what I please.

But, okay, maybe that would indeed look clumsy. I scrapped the formal invitation idea and had the particulars—who, when, where—printed on the front of a formal note card. It's weightier and nicer than invitation stock anyway, and I dared anyone to tell me I can't write a note inside a note card.

Invitations were Tess's One Perfect Thing—the wedding element for which she and her groom went all out. She's in publishing; he's an architect. Hence, both are particular about design. A book designer crafted the look—or looks, one might say. Each invitation was an original work of art.

I wrote notes to my part of the invitation list, and Future Husband wrote notes to his. This is a pleasant Saturday morning task when you're sending fewer than 30 invitations. Each note reflected the kind of relationship we had with each person or couple. *We hope you will share our day.* Or *Be there or be square.* This was one aspect of wedding preparation I fully enjoyed—connecting with special people.

These days, couples of all ages are generally the ones doing the inviting. Younger couples may still include the parents on the invitation, and today that often means the parents of both the bride and the groom. That's six names on one invitation, assuming no stepparents. Gee, that's democratic. Cluttered, too. Mid-lifers and brave young people are spared this jumble. Everyone they're inviting knows them personally. There's no need to identify any parents.

The invitations were just a nice redundancy. Nearly everyone we invited already knew we were getting married. That was part of the beauty of a short invitation list; it consisted of people with whom we connected more often than once a decade. That also meant there was no need to print reply cards, reply envelopes, hotel information or directions to the ceremony. All that interaction could be easily *and* congenially addressed by phone. We also nixed programs, place cards and menus. Sit with whom you like. What you see is what you eat.

Stationers must hate the simple wedding. I suspect they're the inventors of the two-part wedding, which necessitates two invitations.

Stationers can also get their revenge with announcements. If you're not inviting the multitudes, it's still nice to tell them the news—without having to do hundreds of phone calls or letters. If you're a long-time solo act, it's also fun to shock old acquaintances who don't know the new, domesticated you. Here's where it's nice to involve the parents:

They may like to share the news with their own friends regardless of how well they're known to you. One printed announcement will do for all announcers if it's worded in the past tense: *Marie Jones and Donald Price were wed. . . .*

To several announcements I added personal notes such as *Strange but true!* And with all, we enclosed our engagement photo to satisfy at least visual curiosity about whom we wed.

"How come *I* didn't get a photo?" said more than one miffed wedding guest after the fact. "But you saw us *live,*" I tried to explain. Still, a photo would have been a nice and easy token to give to those who went to the trouble of joining us.

"What about your thank-you notes?" said the saavy salesperson. So our third and final piece of stationery was a blank note card, for which I yielded to beautifully blind-embossed initials. The excuse for this expense: This would be personal stationery for a lifetime.

"Just your own initials," advised the salesperson. "Thank you notes come from the bride only." Good grief! I capitulated. On her pad, she wrote down the initials of a total stranger. After 46 robust years, SLM was suddenly receiving last rites. Long live SMC . . . whoever that is.

On Invitations . . .
Consider This

• **Let your invitations reflect your image of your wedding.** If you're planning an offbeat party, by all means have some offbeat invitations. You can buy off the shelf, order from a book or work with a stationer on a custom design.

• **Traditional stationery doesn't have to be stodgy.** Find a way to instill a personal touch. And don't overwork the formality: Select a typeface people can actually read. Shun extended wording like *the twenty-eighth of September at six-thirty o'clock. . . .*

• **Identify a stationer who best reflects the style you want.** Traditional stationers don't necessarily do avant-garde very well, and vice versa. Be skeptical of a stationer who claims to be great at anything and everything.

• **Question authority.** Don't feel obliged to do things only "the way things are done." However, be open to advice. Some traditions happen to be practical and smart.

• **Consider handwritten, personal notes.** This works well if your number of invitations is small. Tailor the notes to each guest. It's gratifying for you and the recipient alike.

• **Spend on quality of paper rather than on the number of enclosures.**

• **Including parents' names on invitations is unnecessary and irrelevant.** You and your groom are inviting your own guests.

• **Send announcements.** If your wedding is small, it's a great way to spread the word to the masses. Let parents get in on it, too. It allows them to share their joy with people *they* know and care about.

• **Thank-you stationery is optional.** Of course, thank-you notes are *not* optional. You just have to decide whether to order stationery especially for this purpose.

White Is All Right!:
Your Attire

B arbra?
    From the magazine rack near the supermarket checkout counter blushes a woman shimmering in tulle. It's none other than Barbra Streisand in full gossamer glory, with flowing veil and overflowing bodice. There are no rules for what a mid-life bride can or cannot do, but. . . .

You, Barbra, and every other bride have the right to do as you please with your wedding—especially when it comes to the way you look. Nothing in your wedding plan is more personal.

Mid-lifers are challenged to look bridal on the one hand and "age-appropriate" on the other. Fortunately, that mix is not the contradiction it used to be. A generation or two ago, when brides were meant to be virginal, they were supposed to *look* virginal, too. Although today's young bride hardly tries to appear pure, she at least strives to look sweet. For mid-life brides, even "sweet" is a stretch. And besides, who needs it? In myriad and wonderful ways, your bridal image can blend the sophistication of your years with the barely diminished bounce of your youth. More than the younger bride, you can look confident and "knowing." You can portray the woman of experience—in the nicest meaning of the word.

There's still plenty of room for getting your look wrong. But the bottom line is: Be happy with your look. Barbra, most of all, looked happy.

I was in Boston for a meeting that had suddenly been postponed by a day. I had a rare gift: free time. And it was about time I found something to wear on my wedding day, which was merely . . . *ten weeks away!* At home, I'd already looked in a few "regular" stores for a "regular" dress or suit—something sufficiently bridal that could be worn on subsequent occasions. It's pretty common for a mature or second-time bride to go for a practical investment instead of a one-shot expense that will hog the closet forever. So far, nothing had fit the bill. One elegant suit in a buttery satin drew me close, then gave me pause. It whispered "second wedding." That's fine, of course. But once in my life, I would have a wedding *dress.*

I'd heard of this famous Boston bridal salon. Heck, why not go see? I was hardly shopping for a gown—much less from some fancy shop— but maybe I could get some inspiration. At the least, I could relive an experience of two decades earlier, when my buddy Donna asked me to go downtown with her to look for a dress for her wedding. I'd never been in the hallowed sanctum of a bridal salon before, and now I was worthy. *It's okay; I'm with the bride.* Like a six-year-old, I sat mute with awe watching Donna metamorphose into one Cinderella after another. I could barely imagine how she felt.

Now I could find out. I trudged for a mile across snowy Boston Common and arrived at the salon's door. One cannot just walk in; one must buzz.

"Do you have an appointment?" asked the intercom.

Well, no.

"I'm sorry, we see customers only by appointment."

By the time I trudged back to my hotel, I was sufficiently miffed to call and make an appointment. Can't turn *me* away that handily.

Back at the salon, I fought an apologetic tone and inquired with head held high:

"Do you have something suitable for a mature bride?"

You've got to love the salesperson who doesn't bat an eye.

"When is your wedding?"

May 25th.

"This year?"

Cute.

Long after my wedding, I would learn that women in their forties are no strangers to bridal salons. And yes, we typically squeeze the turnaround time. According to the manager of a custom salon in Dallas, we tend to rush in saying, "He asked, and we're doing it!"

"Since March, I've sold dresses to three older brides," she says in April. "They're all getting married by July." At the same time, her younger customers were shopping for weddings that wouldn't take place for nearly a year. As she spoke, a 40-something woman tried on a cool linen sheath with scalloped trim for a wedding a month away. There was no time for a dress made from scratch. She'd have to settle for what was in stock and a quick tuck here and there.

Most mid-lifers still opt for alternative wear—evening dresses, sundresses, dressy suits, dressy pants. Some mid-lifers even select from the bridesmaid rack. "I didn't want to do the big gown again," says Elaine, "or the expensive price tag that went along with it."

And who needs to be Cinderella when one can be the Fairy Godmother? At a young couple's wedding, there's no mistaking the most captivating woman in the place. Her strut is regal. Her head is high. Her gaze is assured. The bride may be the fairest of them all, but Mama is the diva of the day.

So is the mid-life bride. We're every bit as knowing and confident, and we should dress accordingly.

Still, if you previously married in tie-dye or leather, or if you've never married at all, you may be lured by that white-lace chance of a lifetime. That's fine. Instead of the big gown, you'll probably aim for the smooth sheath, if your figure permits, or a tea-length hemline. But nearly every salesperson can tell one tale of a mid-lifer who's gone Scarlett O'Hara all the way.

Color is a non-issue. Once upon a time, first-timers wore white, while second-timers wore shades of ivory or champagne more "appropriate" to their recycled condition. Today, brides of all ages wear whatever color suits their taste or skin tone. In nontraditional wear, some brides go past shades of white to pale pastels or even vivid hues.

"I hope you'll wear white," said Future Husband. I preferred off-white but kept my mouth shut. Since he's not a fashion or interior designer, off-white could pass for white.

Playing Dress-up-Barbie was an amusing diversion for a snowy Boston afternoon, even if the woman in the mirror never existed and never would. Ruling out ruffles, bows, puffs and poufs helped whittle down the choices and the time spent. Nonetheless, every remaining dress looked demure. I couldn't pass for demure and didn't want to. And even if I'd married in my twenties, I'm sure I would have bypassed the "uniform," to my parents' dismay, in favor of maybe an African *bubu* or gauzy Indian cotton. Hillary Clinton's wedding dress was on the order of the latter. Times have changed since 1975, and so has Hillary. If she were to marry again, I imagine she'd choose something quite different. In an outfit, I mean. . . .

But darn it if the saleswoman didn't find The Dress before I made it out the door. It was understated and grown-up. At least it would be once the train was hacked off to ballerina length. Though I'd pictured myself in something sleek, the rustle of crinoline got to me. The low back clinched it. I was Betty Davis in *All About Eve*.

My out was geography. I couldn't readily travel to Boston for fittings. Foiled again: The salon had recently branched out, and a new store had opened in Virginia. It was just minutes from my job! The Dress could be shipped there for my fittings! I could rush over on my lunch hour! Shoot!

Before I signed on the dotted line, I called my mother long-distance. Like most mid-lifers, I was shopping for my wedding dress without her. But unlike many, I had no friend, sister, or daughter with me. Did The Dress sound okay? Should I get it? Mom expressed only confidence in my judgment. At rare moments, being in charge is lonely.

"Cut off this gorgeous train? Why?" The seamstress clutched the skirt and nearly wept.

I'm too old for a train.

"You're not!"

Thanks, but no. And take this cluster of flowers off my butt, too.

Losing patience with this process, I settled the rest of my ensemble in a flash. I selected shoes and a small, beautifully beaded cap with one drawback—a long veil.

"We only *do* long veils," said the salesperson.

Not anymore. The seamstress and I ditched yards of fairy-tale tulle and fashioned a soft, elegant pouf, and I was out of there. "Wow, I've never had a customer make decisions so fast!" exclaimed the salesperson.

"Older brides are more concise," says a more knowledgeable salon manager. "They're only trying to please themselves, not their mothers or their friends."

The next day, I picked up some panty hose, congratulating myself for matching my skirt color and buying an extra emergency pair. Finally, I reserved my mother's pearl earrings.

Done!!

"Now, what about your trousseau?" asked my mother.

Trousseau?? I conjured up a '50s nightmare of a jacket dress in pastel bouclé with matching pumps, white gloves, and a pillbox hat. I'll find something that's already in the closet, Mom. Something *Simple*.

The Dress was my one unintended wedding extravagance. I spent twice as much money as I'd planned and wound up with an unmistakable wedding dress that could never be worn again.

On the other hand, I looked fabulous.

"Don't worry," said Future Husband. "I probably spent that much on my suit." I had talked him out of wearing his tuxedo. As the only male member of the wedding party, I thought he might look odd as the only person among the celebrants in black tie. In retrospect, that was probably a meaningless concern. Yet even better was his Plan B—a tailor-made Italian silk suit so delectable that a female wedding guest asked permission to feel him.

Clothing the rest of the wedding party was a snap. Like most mid-lifers, I rob bridal salons of the profits of dressing a big backup team of bridesmaids. I gave Heather the freedom to wear whatever she pleased. That's a bridesmaid's dream come true.

Thirteen-year-olds in particular welcome any opportunity to make personal choices. And this bride welcomed every opportunity not to make more choices than she had to.

"What color?" asked Heather. There was that color thing again. People kept inquiring about "my colors" for the wedding, and darned if I knew. After her mother vetoed her choice of a black sequined number with spaghetti straps, Heather chose pink lace. *Voilà* my color.

I had no idea how the full wedding party would look until the Big Mo. Heather's long pink dress looked great next to Future Husband's blue suit but not so hot with his yellow tie, which in turn didn't go with the pink boutonniere I'd chosen. But I suspect the three of us looked more coordinated than another mid-life wedding party I heard about: The groom was in tan, the best man was in navy and the bride's son was in green. *Laissez-faire* has its limits.

Annette and Bob remembered to tell *some* of their guests their attire should be casual. They showed up in everything from jeans to Sunday best.

A downside of wedding planning is that there's no point in taking notes on what to do better "next time."

Months after the wedding, I returned to the salon to show the seamstress my pictures, as I'd promised. Someone new was at the reception desk, and—I am not kidding—she assumed out loud that I wanted to share pictures of my *daughter's* wedding. Fortunately, I have a sense of humor. However, at bridal salon college, Tact 101 should *not* be an elective.

Husband has worn his suit several times since the wedding. The Dress hangs in a blimp of a bag in the closet of my childhood bedroom. When the sentiment wears off a little more, I expect I'll sell it. For certain, no daughter will ever wear it. Should I have a big 25th anniversary party, I doubt it will look age-appropriate when I'm 71. Then again, 25 years ago I hardly thought that I'd occasionally wear a miniskirt today.

My bridal ensemble memento for the ages is an exquisite pillow crafted by a family friend from my leftover train and butt flowers. Take note, Martha Stewart. Another memento is my headpiece. One day maybe Heather will wear it—plain, poufed or veiled. Meantime, I'll plop it on my head once in a while, look in the mirror and smile.

On Your Attire . . .
Consider This

• **Forget what others may expect.** Choose your attire on the basis of taste, wedding venue, practicality, and price—nothing else.

• **But consider the groom.** Is it *his* first time? Quiet as it's kept, men have wedding fantasies, too. His may include a vision of a bride in a long white gown and veil. You can reconsider your choice, compromise or negotiate. However, you have the tie-breaking vote.

• **If you're going traditional, go for mature.** No matter how well preserved you are in face or physique, you do not look like a 20-year-old. Period. Sporting a dress that's too *jeune fille* will only make you look older by contrast. Shun anything cute—bows, puffed sleeves, ruffles, wispy chiffon and tremendously poufed skirt. Steer toward elements of elegance: simple lines, satin, lace. Keep detail to a minimum.

• **Don't confine yourself to not-quite-white.** Rules of color are dead. No matter how many times you've wed, wear screaming white if it pleases you.

• **For nontraditional wear, think out of the box.** Any look goes—church, nightclub or garden party. Unlike very young brides, you can carry off sultriness and glamour without looking like you're playing dress-up. Dare to think side slits up to the knee, low back, a *bit* of cleavage, stiletto heels—provided they suit your body. In color, you can go beyond variations of white.

Pastels are great. Vivid colors don't say "bride" to me, but if they say "bride" to you, go ahead.

• **Be a bride!** If you choose to be wed in "plainclothes," make sure you look like the bride and not just another guest. Spice up your look with a strand of pearls, a veil on your pillbox or a sumptuous corsage.

• **Work with the pros and cons of your figure.** Keep your bosom covered if it's bony, matronly or threatening to turn to crepe. Also keep covered if your neck or chin line is on the decline. It's a rare mid-lifer who still has tight upper arms. Take a good look at them before you choose something sleeveless. Then don't shake the salt. On the positive side: If you're still narrow of waist, midriff, or hip, let your outfit flaunt it. If you ever had great legs, you still do! Think about showing them off.

• **On your head, go with less rather than more.** A simple hat, band, comb, clip or cluster of flowers is more grown-up and less virginal than a veil. If you're set on having a veil, consider a short one. In hats, think small and structured rather than huge and floppy.

• **Don't feel obliged to have something old, something new, something borrowed, something blue.** This is yet another unnecessary tradition. It's a nice sentiment, however. Follow it if it appeals to you. No, you are not the "something old."

• **Coordinate the wedding party.** It's great to give members of a small wedding party ample freedom to wear what they choose. But prevent a complete lack of order. Give the members some broad guidelines concerning color and degree of formality.

Get Rid of This Wrinkle:
On Beauty

G rowing old gracefully.
  To mid-lifers of yesteryear, the adage meant forsaking shorts, putting on a loose dress, and taking comfort in a new role as a cuddly, cookie-baking grandmother. Growing old gracefully isn't dead, but for our generation it's taken on new meaning.

In our thirties, we were alarmed at our first sightings of a gray hair, laugh line, or ripple of cellulite. Today, some dozen sightings later, we still don't like these developments, but they no longer freak us out. We strive to counteract, cover up or postpone our inevitable decline. Yet we accept what we can't change. We value ourselves most for the beauty we hold within. That's growing old gracefully for today's modern woman.

Unless she's about to attend a class reunion. Or her own wedding. Grace, take a hike.

Help me get rid of this wrinkle! Facial practitioners and makeup artists are accustomed to hearing this plea from the bride past her prime. Looking youthful remains an objective for brides of every age. We all feel "new," in a sense, and for the Big Mo, we want to look it, too.

"Brides should start their skin regimen six months in advance of their wedding," advises a beauty consultant at a bridal show. She's talking about the average bride, I gather. Six months in advance, many mid-lifers don't even know marriage is in the cards. And if we do, six months' effort will barely help.

I once sat front row, center, at a panel discussion on the beauty secrets of Senegalese women—arguably the most beautiful women on the planet. It was disheartening to learn that their regimens start in infancy.

It didn't dawn on me to get serious until two months before my wedding, and I had an uphill battle. In skin, I have the attributes—the wrong ones—of women both young and old. Faint lines are showing up around my mouth and across my forehead. Bags sit under my eyes when I'm tired. Crow's feet of the future mock me when I smile. Late in the day, an oily gleam blooms between my brows. Most annoying are the occasional pimples that broadcast my dietary sins. They may heal quickly, but the scars they leave behind are forever.

I recruited my mother as my skin regimen buddy. "By the time of the wedding," I told her, "people will whisper *She's the mother of the bride? You're kidding!*"

"Ha," said Mom.

"And then they'll look at me and say, *That middle-aged man is marrying this young girl? How disgusting!*"

"I doubt that," said Mom. Unnecessarily.

I wanted no beauty consultant. I'd never had a facial, and I feared "After" might look worse than "Before." After weeks of puncturing, kneading, steaming, creaming, and Zamboni-ing by some charlatan, I suspected that all I'd have to show for it would be a ravaged mug and a fat bill. I'm not sure what a facial peel is, but I'm sure I don't want to know.

I knew what I mainly had to do anyway: get ascetic. For two months, no nuts, chocolate, or fried anything crossed my lips. I cut back on caffeine and forced down water. I kept up the usual cleansing, toning and moisturizing, and remembered to exfoliate a couple of times a week. The best thing I could have done in the name of beauty was quit my job. Overwork and stress make you ugly like nothing else. Short of that, I ordered myself to bed an hour earlier than usual.

Seeing a professional is a fine idea if you have a practitioner you've grown to trust and a clear—no pun intended—expectation of the outcome. You'll have to decide whether "six months" is a rip-off or a worthwhile investment.

Like mid-life faces, mid-life bodies are past their peak On average, today's mid-lifer is in much better shape than the mid-lifer of a generation ago. In high school, some of you got out of gym class at every opportunity. However, fitness centers and aerobics classes got trendy while we were still young enough to benefit substantially. If you really benefited, parts of the older you may look better than they did in your youth. My toothpick ankles, for example, are a distant memory.

Forget about total physical transformation. Fast-track weight loss makes older skin sag. Fad diets and sudden extremes in your fitness regimen can damage your health. Be yourself and love her. After all, *you* are the woman your groom wants to marry. What more affirmation do you need?

To surprise her husband, my parents' neighbor had liposuction performed on her thighs. Due to a mishap of anesthesia, she didn't make it off the operating table alive.

"Why did she do it?" asked the mournful husband. "I loved her just the way she was."

Just strive to be a little better at being yourself. From the moment you say "Yes," commit to a reasonable food and fitness routine.

Being just a little better is a good rule of thumb for your wedding makeup, too.

By age 30, most women grow weary of the makeup experimentation that began in puberty. You've lost interest in the 30-color eye shadow kit. You've become set in a makeup routine. Stroke, dab, brush, swipe, and you're out of the house. When, after 15 years or so, your Damson Plum shadow is discontinued, you'll sigh and find something comparable.

Is your makeup the best it could ever be? Probably not. Is it good enough? Probably so. Marriage doesn't compel most mid-lifers to seek a whole new look. And Mom isn't going to drag you to Bloomingdale's against your will for a makeover.

All brides are wisely advised to take a soft and subtle approach to their makeup. Looking virginal is unnecessary, but so is looking like a hooker. Yet mid-lifers shouldn't take subtlety too far. For one thing, with less blush and glow coming from Mother Nature, you could probably use a little help. For another, you're striving to look womanly, not demure. Depending on skin tone, you can go beyond pale pastels to somewhat stronger tones like rose or lavender. Unlike younger brides, you can wear fuchsia lipstick without looking like you've been poking in the jam jar. But stop short of the deepest and most fluorescent hues. No peacock blue, please.

All of the above goes for your nail color, too.

When mid-life brides do go to a makeup artist, they know what they want. "They'll say from the start *Don't make my eyebrows too dark* or *don't use this color*," says one consultant. "If we don't achieve what they want, they'll go elsewhere. They don't waste time."

Avoid taking the opportunity of your wedding to do anything radical. If you normally wear no makeup, wear a little for a change—but don't do Tammy Faye Baker. Likewise, if you're usually quite colorful, toning things down may be a good idea, but don't emulate a novice entering the convent. Again, your husband expects to marry *you*. As you walk down the aisle, he shouldn't wonder *Who the heck is that?* Most of all, he shouldn't dislike what he sees.

While mid-lifers rarely change makeup, many want an occasional change of hairstyle. And nothing takes the years off as quickly and thoroughly as a hairstyle update. Most brides, regardless of age, look best with hairdos that are simple and off the face. For mid-lifers, adding lift to the hair achieves a cost-effective face lift. Choose a modern style that works across generational borders. If it's too MTV, your face will look older by contrast.

Wear your hair long if you like a droopy face. When I'm queen, women over 35 with hair beyond shoulder length will be subject to arrest. For their own good. Yes, Goldie Hawn and Cher still look fabulous. But given a serious pruning, they'd make you say *Wow*. . . .

An exception: Long hair may work beautifully if you're the Earth Mother type—a "flower grownup," if you will, letting it all hang out. Accompanied by the appropriate attire and attitude, long hair can evoke a noble, natural woman rather than an aging chick.

You'll probably make no more than a small change in your usual style. But if you want anything radically new, you'll need time to try it way in advance. After all, you can't undo a cut or chemical treatment as quickly as you can undo eye liner.

Got a little gray? Keep it or color it. But if you're more gray than not, you'll only look comical to your guests if you're suddenly a solid brunette. Proudly keep that gray, and have your stylist make it shine.

Wisely, I went to my hair stylist 10 days in advance of the wedding. The time lapse ensured that my hair wouldn't be too skimpy to be grabbed by the combs of my head piece. I wanted nothing special— just my usual minimalist cut. Yet this was special; it was my Wedding Cut. Seemed like something ought to be said.

"I'm getting married next week," I mumbled. The stylist made minimal cooing noises, and I'm grateful.

On Beauty . . .
Consider This

• **Start your wedding beauty regimen** *yesterday*. Get rest, guzzle water, eat right, and counteract stress. Exercise with an emphasis on firmness rather than thinness. Two words: upper arms.

• **Don't aim for total transformation.** Aim for incremental improvements.

• **Don't work on a suntan.** Older skin can turn to leather in a hurry. Wear sunscreen.

• **Beware of facials.** Get facial treatments only if you're experienced with them and know what results you can expect.

Your face may need at least a week to recover from a treatment, so plan ahead.

• **Avoid radical changes in makeup and hairdo.** Don't do anything extreme unless you have ample time to try it and change it back. If your hairstyle is stuck in the '70's, consider at least a modest update. It's a quick and easy road to the fountain of youth.

• **Be subtle—but not too subtle—with your makeup.** Help Mother Nature by adding a bit more color and glow.

• **Note to some of you: Do not add any more makeup whatsoever!** I wish you knew who you are.

• **Spend a few extra minutes on makeup and hair.** Even if you're sticking with your usual routine, spend a little more time getting it perfect before the Big Mo. You'll be a bigger focus of attention than usual. And there will be photographs to remind you—for a lifetime—of any flaws.

• **Condition your hair early and often.**

• **Almost a rule: If there's no space between your shoulders and your hair, chop it.** At minimum, harness it into a neat bun, twist or braid.

• **Consider suggestions, but remember who's boss.** When working with makeup artists and hair stylists, it helps if they're probably your age or younger and not likely to push you around.

• **And the No. 1 beauty tip is: Spend a lot of quality time with the groom.** Stick with a beauty regimen *after* the wedding, too. Preserve that glorious look as long as possible.

The Woman Giveth
This Woman: On Vows
and Ceremony

"One of the drawbacks of not having children is knowing there's no one to look after me when I'm old," I said to Future Husband.

"Maybe we'll take care of each other," he replied.

An endearing sentiment. Ridiculous and frightful, too. At the time, we'd known each other for only two weeks. But I kept those words in my back pocket. If there's any substance to them down the road, I figured, he's a keeper.

Vows are born not at the altar but on that long, meandering aisle leading up to it.

"I know a lot of people write their own vows nowadays," said Future Husband down the road, "but I'd like our vows to be traditional." I was disappointed for half a minute. That's how long it took me to realize that not writing vows meant One Less Thing to Do! Later, it further dawned that I'd probably be pen-tied anyway. I couldn't imagine coming up with anything much less cliché than *Roses are red.* . . . Nor could I imagine sharing an intensely personal dialogue with my partner in front of other people.

Writing your own vows became hot in the '60s. If you were establishment enough to marry your soul mate in the first place, the least you could do was unleash the individual within and say something original. Any woman can take "this man." But only you can take "James, who makes my heart smile." Transcending fad, original vows remain popular 30 years later among people who went to Woodstock, as well as people who were conceived there. Their weddings often include at least a brief personal statement, spoken either by the minister or between the bride and groom. The practice stands to reason: No commitment is more personal than marriage.

Future Husband's plea for traditional vows had more to do with stage fright than with his perception of our writing abilities. The less he had to utter at the moment of truth, the better. Most of all, he wanted to feel he was "really" being married. He needed the trappings, from traditional vows to cake. More than I'd suspected, I needed some of that, too. Maybe it was another first-timer thing. *To have and to hold* says marriage. *To fulfill your days and nights* says Barry White.

But perhaps we were atypical of mid-lifers. Although my own wedding was history, curiosity implored me to check out a Bridal Expo— a carnival of hawkers of everything remotely bridal. Amid the jewelers, florists, stationers, caterers, cake bakers, tuxedo renters, bridal gown sellers, wedding coordinators, photographers, videographers, limousine services, disc jockeys and one brass quartet, darned if I didn't stumble upon the booth of an ordained minister. A specialist in composing "non-denominational wedding vows," she told me that mid-life couples are more into nontraditional vows than her younger clients.

"The older bride knows and can speak to why she's marrying *this* man," she explained. "Older couples also have a stronger sense of what their personal values are. They want to incorporate them in their ceremony."

Mid-life brides and grooms also feel kind of like born-again adults. Odds are, you've encountered more valleys on life's road than younger couples, simply by virtue of traveling the road longer. You may thus be doubly motivated to write your own vows—not only to rejoice in the life that lies ahead but also to kiss the past good-bye. Whether you've suffered through a bad marriage, 20 years of workaholism or a long period of loneliness, now you've recovered. With marriage, life isn't beginning so much as it's beginning anew. And someone wants to share that with you! It's a powerful feeling—perhaps a religious experience for some of you—and you want to put it in words.

One can take this approach too far, however. My mother gave me a book filled with a potpourri of traditional and nontraditional vows. The suggested vows for the person "in recovery" sound like the vows of last year's poster child for the Wretch Association. Hearing these vows, the Dearly Beloved of the second party would surely stage a kidnapping for his or her own good.

Neither Future Husband nor I had a church or a pastor. Still, we wanted a pastor to perform the ceremony. A judge wouldn't evoke the right spirit. We were bonding in love, not in business.

Another of the Wedding Elves told me instantly who would perform the ceremony. I hadn't seen him in a number of years. In fact, I'd never been in his presence on a regular basis. Calvin was a longtime family friend as well as an ordained minister. Mentored by the minister who married my parents, he was remotely linked to my personal history. Although he was a man of the cloth, he always seemed a man of the Earth, firmly rooted in the here and now. Perhaps that's because he'd spent much of his career in social service rather than the pulpit. Whatever the reason, I liked that in a wedding officiant. What I liked most of all was that, in his presence, I'd always felt comfort.

"Calvin lives in Atlanta now," my mother informed me.

Atlanta? That was not in my script. But I knew that as the weather turned warm each year, he traveled north to his summer home. Maybe this time a nice letter would persuade him to pass through New York on his way. On, say, May 25th. I wrote, and he said Yes.

Inasmuch as we wanted traditional vows, we didn't want to commit to any words that didn't ring true for both of us. Future Husband in particular needed a heads-up on what he was about to pledge. He'd never been to an American wedding, let alone been *in* one.

My mother, who normally can't locate a piece of paper an hour after it's been in her hand, reached into some private stash and readily pulled out her own Methodist wedding ceremony. People actually have copies of their own ceremonies! I hadn't a clue. Her vows, along with the slightly updated version our minister planned to use, were poetic in the time-honored way—*for richer, for poorer*—that often triggers a tear or two in the congregation. No doubt about it; this is a wedding.

The vows were refreshingly straightforward. Nothing needed translation. No plighting of troth. These vows were also up to date: No one had to be given away, and certainly no one had to promise to obey. As I would learn from cyberspace, the United Methodist Church declared some years back that marriage is a partnership of equals. To my way of thinking, our vows came from a church with the right idea.

Two incredibly busy mid-lifers I know separately carved out time to write their own vows. They failed, however, to find time to memorize them. On the eve of the wedding, the bride and groom each made a crash effort to learn their lines. It wasn't very successful.

"I don't think anyone noticed besides us," the bride laughs.

Two smarter mid-lifers had their written vows in hand. After he read his vows, she donned her reading glasses to read hers. "*I didn't print mine in large type,*" she remarked to the gathering.

Whether writing vows or parroting them, mid-life couples know what younger couples can only hope they know—that they've got what it takes to stay the course. By now, experience has revealed to us—repeatedly—our strengths and weaknesses. They've been tested. We know what kinds of diversity we can handle and how much. We know love doesn't conquer all without some help from mental toughness.

We also have a pretty realistic idea of what our partners can handle. Indeed, we may be amazed that a sane man will vow to take us, baggage and all. Nonetheless, couples should discuss what they expect to give *and* get from each other long before they arrive at the altar. Some specific understandings may be warranted, and I don't mean kisses for breakfast. To Future Husband, I divulged flat out that my father's illness could be hereditary. Even as I hoped never to be a burden, I also had to know if and how I could count on Future Husband should that be the case. *In sickness and in health* loomed large in my mind. And I've heard stories of a number of husbands—loving and sensitive husbands—who've bailed out in the face of a serious family illness.

To have and to hold. . . . Future Husband muttered this line repeatedly in the weeks before the wedding. As a foreign speaker of English, he contemplated the distinction between "have" and "hold." Mainly, he just liked the way the phrase rolled off the tongue. His careful study of all these American-style vows forced me to look upon them with fresh eyes myself.

Did we need to meet—not *rehearse*, but get together real quick the night before to talk the ceremony over?

"Nah," said Calvin. Even the minister understood: Ain't nothing but a Simple wedding. To Future Husband's great relief, we wouldn't even have to repeat the vows aloud. I would have liked that, but I know how seriously he worries about getting choked up. I let it be. Our only lines would be the Lord's Prayer and "I will."

"You said it in your little girl voice," my mother later remarked with amusement. So much for the diva in the bride.

For as long as you both may live. The words that made me shiver all my life finally gave me extraordinary peace.

On Vows . . .
Consider This

• **Agree to the commitments in your vows with your groom.** Like prenuptial agreements, everything about nuptial agreements must be mutually satisfactory. As a mid-lifer, you probably gave your partner a thorough value check long ago, and you know his values pertaining to wedlock are darn close to your own. Now all you need to do is review those values before putting them into words.

• **Bring religious considerations to the table.** The adage *Never discuss religion or politics* doesn't apply to your marriage ceremony or vows. If your belief system dictates that certain practices must be part of your ceremony, be prepared to discuss what compromises you will or won't make.

• **Figure out what kind of vows are "you."** Traditional? Nontraditional? Original? Some combination? It's up to your taste and perhaps your religious faith. The time and effort required for composing and memorizing original vows may also be factors for consideration.

• **Make sure vows "off the shelf" ring true.** Read them word for word. Depending on your belief system, you may have a variety of ceremonies from which to choose. You can often find written ceremonies in church hymnals and religious bookstores. A wider selection, including secular and nontraditional ceremonies, may be found in mass-market bookstores, libraries or cyberspace. If the ceremony sounds great except for "this one thing," don't hesitate to negotiate with your officiant. He or she may agree to remove a phrase or substitute one word for another.

• **Don't alarm the groom.** If he'll be hearing your original vows for the first time at the altar, it's important not to embarrass him in front of the crowd. Err on the side of caution in revealing personal information.

• **Consult a writer.** If you've got more sentiment than talent, you can have someone assist in writing your original vows. There are ministers and professional writers who can help put your sentiments into words. However, they will need your carefully considered ideas about the messages you want to convey.

• **Use a cheat sheet!** If you don't have time to memorize your original vows, or if you're at the stage of short-term memory loss, there's nothing wrong with carrying a few notes. Clutch them behind your bouquet or tuck them into the sleeve of your dress. Please don't tuck them in your cleavage.

Lohen Who?: On Music

For the Dearly Beloved, the typical wedding processional is a setup. For a good half hour, as the guests take their seats and the mothers are ushered in, you're lulled with soft, lilting tones by Handel or Bach. Delicate music continues to play as the wedding party floats up the aisle, the ushers roll out that long white thing, the flower girl oh-so-gently tosses petals. Then:

BUM BUH-BUH-BUH BUM BUM BUM BUM.

When I was a child and thoughts of marriage were scary, that organ-pounding opening to "Here Comes the Bride" would nearly drive me from the church. I may be grown, but that tune still sends a mild shudder through my veins.

"That tune" is the Bridal Chorus from *Lohengrin*, a Wagnerian opera? Wedding planning is educational.

Call it what you will, a tune that tenses up the bride sounds like a poor choice for her processional. Yet for me, it was the only choice. Let the high school graduates march to Beethoven. Let the second-time brides step to Kenny G. But give me *Lohengrin*——as we insiders call it for short——tension and all. And for the recessional, give me Mendelssohn.

These choices were woefully unimaginative, but they offered two strong advantages: No music says "wedding" the way these two pieces do. And given the universe of great music out there, the job of screening and selecting anything else didn't appeal to me one bit.

Mid-lifers are all over the map with their wedding music, picking anything from standard fare to utmost avant-garde. A second-timer often chooses music the way she chooses attire, going in any direction *but* the direction she went before. Regardless of marital history, many mid-lifers strive for individual expression in their music. You've still got a touch of the rebel in you.

Yet the rebel has evolved: In the '60s, you might have chucked Mendelssohn for Sly and the Family Stone. Today, you might chuck Mendelssohn for Tchaikovsky. It's not that your old taste in music has died; it's just that it's broadened. If back in the day, you were into rhythm & blues or acid rock, you still are. But perhaps now you can find something to like in blues or big-band jazz, too, even if you're still drawing the line at, say, hip-hop or country.

If there was one genre most of us tuned out in our youth, it was classical. Classical was stodgy and old, and the high school string ensemble was hardly the social "A" list. Saturday nights, I could be at some house party getting down to Junior Walker or James Brown. Then on Sunday mornings around 11 A.M.——"dawn"——I'd get blasted awake by the Mormon Tabernacle Choir or the Robert Shaw Chorale at utmost decibels, thanks to my father. Painful.

Since those days, many of us have grown to appreciate classical music. We can even "name that tune" when we hear popular fare like *Bolero* or *The Four Seasons*. Most classical music is soothing, and we're at a point in life when we need all the soothing we can get. It's also elegant, and if we're planning an elegant wedding, it's a perfect backdrop. Then again, so is Duke Ellington.

A Wedding Elf told me to book Nicola, a friend of a friend and a contralto who sings in the chorus of the Metropolitan Opera. My wedding would have either a great soloist or no soloist at all. The next Wedding Elf told me Nicola should sing "One Hand, One Heart" from *West Side Story*. It's lovely and to the point, and it's not "Oh Promise Me." It also takes me back to age ten, when I wore the original Broadway cast album thin. I almost passed over this for an aria from *Madame Butterfly* until it dawned on me that the heroine of the opera gets ditched by her man.

"What about 'Jesu, Joy of Man's Desiring?' " asked my mother. "That's one of your father's favorites."

Sure. I added a second solo to the plan. If there was one thing that still caught my father's fading attention, it was music. And "Jesu" is a gorgeous melody to boot. Satisfying yourself often means satisfying someone you love as well.

At her wedding, Tess opted for audience participation—a simple yet out-of-the-box idea. Standing at the front of the church, her full-throated brother led the Dearly Beloved in some good, old familiar hymns.

Future Husband—who even likes to *wake up* to classical music—delightedly took charge of the rest of the music for our ceremony. With my wedding script in one hand and a pile of CD's in the other, he pieced together the score, summoning Bruch, Vaughan Williams, Chopin, Beethoven and, in a personal spirit of nationalism, Edvard Grieg.

Some selections would be played by the soloist's accompanist on piano. Most were chosen with a violin in mind. Both of us love classical strings. A Wedding Elf said string quartet, but a single violin seemed simple and sufficient, not to mention less expensive. Finding the violinist was my job, and in New York, that should be as easy as jaywalking in midtown Manhattan at midday. In other words, you may have to work at it a bit, but you will succeed. Alas, my contacts weren't as bountiful as I'd expected. I nailed our violinist just two nail-munching weeks ahead of time. "Here's the list of music. Talk to the pianist." It would be my least efficient wedding accomplishment—among several worthy contenders.

For modern-day ceremonies, the music may range from somber to

lighthearted. But at receptions past and present, the music says nothing
but PARTY!

The gap between mid-life reception music and young reception
music is not as wide as one might think. After all, the music should aim
to appeal to the whole gathering, from grandma to grandchild. Still,
your own generation may be the dominant group present. Hence, the
music you like will dominate, too.

Now: What do you like? The radio industry's got your number.
Nouveau categories like classic country and AUC—adult urban contemporary—stand for y-o-u. These stations play the music of any of
several genres, but what they have in common is the pursuit of the ears
and incomes of baby boomers. They don't play the ear candy that's
popular with teenagers or Generation X. Nor do they play your parents'
postwar favorites. Mostly they play pop—today's pop, meaning Elton
John or Whitney Houston. Or they play hits of the '60s and '70s. In
your honor, this music has been upgraded from "oldies" to "classics."
Some stations play "light jazz," which is akin to light beer. Some stations
play combinations of the above.

Mid-life music is ideal reception music. You and most of your guests
like it, and it neither irritates nor bores anybody else.

"Many older couples like to add a little young music, too," said a
seasoned wedding disc jockey. "It makes them feel with-it." In the '90s,
the music and moves of the Electric Slide and the Macarena got so
popular with mid-lifers, I suspect young people dropped them in a
hurry.

Nostalgia is a factor in mid-life reception music. According to the
disc jockey: "Couples generally pick music from the good times in their
lives, not necessarily from the young times."

Therein lie a few potential mid-life quandaries: Your good times
may have been the '80's; your groom's may have been the '70's. Maybe
the good times were the '70's for both of you, but you were into
Roberta Flack and he was into the Rolling Stones. After all, unless
you're one of those longtime couples, your paths may have followed
distinctly different routes before they crossed.

The good news is that, unlike your choice of processional, dress, or invitations, your reception music can embrace variety.

When your after-party is in the same space as your solemn ceremony, music helps mark the distinction between phases one and two. We did it with pianists: In with the jazz artist, out with the classical. Live music was all we ever considered, by the way. It was our treat to our music-loving selves, and the outdoor setting seemed to make it all the more appropriate.

I spared Future Husband a complete '60's R&B retrospective and suggested romantic and jazzy ballads of the past and present. AUC plus the songs my mother hums. A Wedding Elf said the artist had to be none other than Grenoldo, a charismatic pianist and song stylist who's performed at my friend Delores's poetry readings. A renegade Wedding Elf envisioned the Count Basie Orchestra with Luther Vandross, but never mind.

"Grenoldo moved to North Carolina," Delores informed me.

Heck. I called Grenoldo, gently fussed, and asked him for the name and number of a reasonable local facsimile. Kenny came to the rescue.

Many couples have "their" song. We didn't, but a couple of songs by Sarah Vaughan and Joe Cocker remind me of our earliest, headiest days together, and I included them on the play list. As I heard Kenny play the opening chords of one of "my" songs out of the past, I couldn't help but embrace my new husband for a dance on the patio. Days later, it dawned on me that my song was from a time when I knew someone else. Didn't matter. Now it belongs to me and my husband.

There's a ribbon in the sky for our love.

On Music . . .
Consider This

• **Pick a musical style that suits your ceremony.** You've got three basic categories to choose from: There are the time-honored wedding classics—*Lohengrin*, Mendelssohn, "Ave Maria," and the like. There are other classical pieces by the likes of Handel and Mozart that are less common as wedding fare and at least as beautiful. And of course, you've got the whole range of contemporary and avant-garde music, ranging from solemn to frivolous. Feel free to mix styles, perhaps with a gradual lightening up from start to finish. Just be careful not to turn the ceremony into a joke. *Fifty Ways to Leave Your Lover* is a non-starter.

• **Feel free to repeat selections from your last wedding.** You may feel some old standards are important to any wedding. Repeating more personal selections, on the other hand, may be too reminiscent of the last time around.

• **Know the difference between classic music and dated music.** Avoid "We've Only Just Begun," for example, unless you're having a deliberately retro wedding, go-go boots and all.

• **Feel free to honor another loved one.** Include a piece of music that's a favorite of a parent or child, for example.

• **For a touch of class at the reception, use live music.** Hiring one or two musicians is no more expensive than hiring a disc jockey. For a big reception, however, you made need a full band with amplifiers so the music can be heard above the crowd.

• **If your style is more casual than classy, go with a disc jockey.** That's especially fun if your musical theme is oldies. If your setting is a cozy living room, select some CDs and enlist a volunteer to keep them running.

• **Reconcile musical selections with your groom.** You two probably have roughly overlapping tastes in music. Focus on areas of compatibility in making your selections. Avoid areas of clear divergence. If the two of you have a song, by all means include it, even if it's kind of silly.

• **For a unique sound, consider alternative instruments.** How about a violin-flute-guitar trio? For a tranquil touch, think sitar.

• **Think about engaging the gathering in singing a song almost everyone knows.**

• **Select musicians or a disc jockey proficient in the primary genre you want.** They should also have the flexibility to play other styles. Suggest a few specific songs or artists. Let them expand the play list from there. Keep in mind: They have more wedding experience than you do. They know how to respond to the crowd.

~

No Nosegays: On Flowers
and Froufrou

My parents' backyard is more than a yard. It's Frank's vision. Frank wasn't doing a landscaping job so much as he was fulfilling a commission as meaningful as the ceiling of the Sistine Chapel. *The rhododendron must go here.* Sometime later, his wife fed us enough lasagna, roast chicken and pie at her kitchen table to kill an army. For my seventh birthday party, his daughter-in-law baked a sumptuous whipped cream cake that my mother recalls with passion to this day.

Forty years later, Mom and I sit in Frank's "chapel" conferring with his granddaughter, keeper of the floral side of the family business. Like nearly every other wedding idea, the choice of florist was a sentimental one, rooted in my personal history.

As a younger bride, I wouldn't have known the names of most of the flowers we looked at in the books. Now I know quite a few, and I know my favorites. Still, there was the chore of deciding which among the favorites to choose and how to combine them.

"What are your colors?" asked the florist.

Again with the colors. Well, the bridesmaid's wearing pink. So with pinks and complementary colors in mind, we chose a big arrangement for the buffet, tiny vases for the tables, two buckets to represent the altar, a corsage for my mother, boutonnieres for the men, a wreath for the bridesmaid's hair, my bouquet, the bridesmaid's bouquet—called a nosegay, I learned—a cluster of flowers to top the wedding cake, a little greenery to hang on the porch posts and the buffet tent and a couple of rented shrubs to camouflage the stationary garbage cans.

Another notion of simplicity down the drain.

Perhaps the flower order could pass for simple, considering that the flowers were our only form of decoration. Mid-lifers tend to shun froufrou in their weddings, especially if it's gimmicky. No arches or balloons, no columns or candelabra, no champagne fountains. I have no idea what wedding bubbles are; I merely saw them advertised. But I'll bet mid-lifers don't do that, either.

Whatever props we do have are real. Silk flowers, electric unity candles and plastic toasting glasses are out. So are fake rings for the ring bearer, if we have a ring bearer at all. If real costs more than fake, we'll simply do less of the real if need be. Our props are also likely to be innovative. One couple gave their at-home buffet a personal touch with their collection of antique sterling. For evening weddings, one can go wild with an assortment of candles.

Some props are more than froufrou. They're practical. And thank goodness, other people knew the drill better than I did.

"I bought you a cake serving set," said my mother.

Cake servers? Oh, yeah, good idea.

"I got you a guest book," said Donna.

Guest book? Great.

"What are your colors?" asked the caterer. She instantly read my weary expression and recommended white tablecloths, white napkins, white plates, white tent and white chairs. Perfect.

Then there's the little souvenir stuff: printed matchbooks, swizzle sticks, napkins. All too cliché and unnecessary. Napkins are at least useful. But promoting smoking is passé, and so is scotch on the rocks. "Older couples don't order the extra stuff," a stationer confirmed. Fortunately, there are some modern innovations on souvenirs. Some young couples give their guests T-shirts on the order of *I went to Beverly and*

John's wedding, and all I got. . . . There's no reason why older couples shouldn't do something equally fun and unpredictable.

I succumbed to Jordan almonds in little sacks with printed ribbons. I've always liked the symbolism.

"It means that, in marriage, one has to take the bitter with the sweet," I explained to my foreign sister-in-law. She heartily confirmed this was true.

A premium chocolatier advertises tiny wedding souvenir boxes containing a dark chocolate and a white one. For us, that would have been symbolism gone too far. But I regret that I didn't honor my guests with something more substantial than a handful of jaw-breaking candies. Maybe I can make up for it on our fifth anniversary. *Dear Guests: We're still together. You didn't waste your time coming to our wedding. So please accept this token.* . . .

It's amazing how so many flowers can lose themselves in the background. Then again, it was Frank's background, lush and green with springtime. One early rhododendron blossom appeared in our honor, or maybe his. The altar was perfect: Just two pedestals with the flower buckets, which included a vivid splash of something blue. I wish I'd had the same drama in my pale bouquet—which I failed to preserve. But I still have a coffin-like box of dry petals and ribbon. I believe it's a commingling of the bouquet, the boutonnieres and the corsage my mother forgot to wear.

"Your mother doesn't even need a corsage," Husband said later. "She looks great."

Corsage, not corset, I explained. My mother enjoyed the compliment nonetheless. Along with the other petals, her corsage will find its way into my keepsake box one day.

On Flowers and Froufrou . . . Consider This

• **Incorporate your favorite blossoms.** Even if you're no expert in horticulture, you know what you like. If the season permits, include your favorites in your bouquet or elsewhere in your decor. If you've got the creative inclination and the time, you can do your own designs. Otherwise, let a pro make your ideas manifest.

• **Dare to be vivid.** As with our makeup, mid-lifers can be bold with floral hues. If your attire is simply designed, your bouquet can be busy with multiple colors and blossoms. Don't shy away from big, in-your-face blossoms like calla lilies and peonies. *Do* shy away from anything too mousy and delicate. "Baby's breath" says it all.

• **Leave nosegays to the very young.** Those little round bouquets look decidedly cute and innocent. You may be cute, too, but . . . reserve nosegays for younger brides, bridesmaids and flower girls.

• **Think about your setting.** If you'll wed barefoot on the beach, carry something wild and natural-looking. If you'll be in a grand cathedral, carry something more elegant and "done."

• **Leave false treatments out of your decor.** No plastic flowers, no artificial anything. Aim for quality rather than abundance. Likewise, leave out youthful gimmicks like balloon arches. If gimmicks are in your nature, be more innovative and grown-up about it.

• **Express your nontraditional side.** Light up the place with lanterns, for example. Display interesting collectibles. Around the room, place pictures of yourself and your partner—in strollers, with hula hoops, wearing tie-dye.

• **Get the Dearly Beloved into the act.** Ask them to bring and light candles. Or have each bring one long-stemmed blossom to place in a community vase.

• **Choose special souvenirs.** Give gifts that are more thoughtful and unique than swizzle sticks. If you're having a small gathering, better-than-average souvenirs may be affordable. Possibilities include note holders, candle holders, napkin rings, bud vases, small boxes—in wood, china, paper, silver plate, glass or anything else that can accommodate your names in subtle calligraphy or engraving. Consult a gift shop for ideas. If you're a Martha Stewart type, consider making the gifts yourself.

~

Eel on a Stick:
Wining and Dining

Champagne, wine, and substantial hors d'oeuvres. That was the plan. Plus wedding cake. Elegant, yet . . . Simple!

Mom locked in the date with a popular caterer, whose food and service were familiar to us and excellent. With Future Husband, we chose from a bunch of yummy menu selections, including one very appropriate find: spinach in triangular pillows of phyllo pastry. Future Husband and I may not have had "our song," but we definitely had our vegetable. On the occasion of our first meeting, when he approached my table in the company cafeteria, I was consumed with one thought: I had spinach stuck in my teeth. Future Husband noticed neither the spinach nor the way I barely moved my lips when I spoke, like a bad ventriloquist. Weeks later, I confessed this embarrassment to him. We've joked about it ever since.

Having small weddings, as mid-lifers tend to do, means we can spend more on quality rather than quantity. It also means we know all our guests well. Since they're mostly our peers, their tastes may be more or less akin to our own. We don't have to cater to the very lowest common denominator of food preferences. Small also means expeditious service: Your guests won't grow weary waiting to be served at their tables or standing on a long buffet line. Party downtime is minimal. And because mid-lifers often steer clear of catering halls and hotels, our wedding menus are open to a wider range of food.

In other words: Goodbye, pale chicken and mushy peas!

Future Husband's relatives were coming from the world capital of plain cuisine. To illustrate: A standard meal in those parts is steamed fish and potatoes. On adventurous occasions, there's parsley on the potatoes. Was there anything special we should include on our menu for them?

"No," he said emphatically. "Let's have what *we* want."

Wow! But he's a true mid-lifer. We're more likely to be daring with our menus than younger couples, especially younger couples whose parents are in charge. Our tastes have expanded over the years. So has our creativity. So has our nerve. Our whims are constrained only by budget.

So you're not going to give in to pot roast just because Uncle Harry is coming. You can do a clambake on the beach or burgers and fries under silver-plate domes. You can do a ham-and-grits breakfast, or you can stick with the vegetarian diet you've followed for 30 years without interruption. You can do a standing rib roast, a Hunan buffet or—as we planned it—a generous sampling of innovative finger food representing a mix of culinary traditions and the caterer's imagination.

Finger food was almost *all* we planned. Months ahead of time, before my wedding vision expanded from tiny to moderate, I had planned to invite local friends only. Ten or twelve guests would have been invited to my parents' home for a brief afternoon reception. Then they'd all go home for dinner.

Though I quickly reconsidered the scope of the guest list, I didn't rethink the food until four days before the wedding. Nearly 50 people were on their way to the wedding from hither and yon. For the people of yon, our wedding wasn't taking a mere afternoon out of their lives. It was a weekend or overnight trek. They weren't going home for dinner; they were going to a hotel in an unfamiliar town. And from us, all they were about to get was a between-meal snack.

In a sweat, I called the caterer. Maybe her people weren't done with the food shopping yet. Please.

"No problem," she said.

We cut out a couple of hors d'oeuvres—not the spinach pillows—and added a serious meal: pecan-encrusted filet of chicken plus some gourmet sides. Phew! I hear it was delicious. Mid-life brides have no more appetite at their weddings than younger brides. We're distracted by the interaction with friends, not to mention the drunken buzz of newlywed fever. I intended to do the smart bridal thing by having a plate set aside for later. I forgot. Elaine was smarter: By making her main reception a day-after brunch, she was relaxed enough to eat.

Incidentally, there's nothing unfestive about chicken when it's encrusted with pecans, layered with ham and cheese in the manner *cordon bleu*, or otherwise made interesting. And unlike red meat, sushi or soybeans, chicken offends hardly anyone. Friend Delores shuns meat, eggs, wheat products and onions. Long ago, I learned to let Delores fend for herself.

From all over the greater New York area, people drive or take the train to my hometown wine store, where the selection is excellent and the prices are better than that. Having our wedding ten minutes from the store was just our dumb luck. Future Husband took charge of the libations, negotiating selections long-distance. Like many modern-day weddings, ours did without a full bar. We offered champagne, wine, fruit punch, sparkling water and a few beers.

Today's mid-lifers know what they like in champagne and wine. We're not all connoisseurs, but most of us have evolved beyond jugs and screw-on caps. We may know we like Merlot a lot. We may know we're not big on Chardonnay. And as hosts, we know the general leaning of our crowd. Unless your crowd happens to be an international wine jury, don't try to impress with some over-the-top budget buster. Forget about oaky overtones, good "nose," the must-have year or the big-name chateau. We've grown to appreciate decent wine, but most people haven't the *goût* to appreciate the high end. Just remember: It's your wedding, not a wine festival.

In an old "Dennis the Menace" cartoon, Joey longingly eyed a wedding cake in a bakery window. "But after the cake is gone," Dennis explained, "you'd still be married." Dennis voiced my sentiments of the time to perfection. The only persuasive elements of marriage were wedding cakes and lingerie showers. Yet I might have married long ago, had I known that bakeries load up brides-to-be with boxes of free cake samples. Mom and I spent a delightful afternoon at her kitchen table indulging in a smorgasbord of free delights—with justification.

When did wedding cake change from white to name-your-color? In the '70's, a few African-American weddings went chocolate. Since then, wedding cakes have broken barriers anew, embracing whims ranging from strawberry pink to lemon yellow. Some of them taste great, I discovered at the kitchen table. But they don't taste "wedding," and they certainly don't look it. Some seem more appropriate for a child's birthday party. But if anyone can have a nontraditional cake, it's the independent mid-lifer. Cheesecake, marzipan cake, carrot cake—anything goes. Shape and decor are as open to your innovation as flavor is.

It took me and Mom little time to zero in on the winner. It was wedding-white, yet far too creamy and decadent to be wedding-predictable. The cake would be topped with flowers. Like many couples these days, we did without the stiff little bride and groom. The cake was served with a huge bowl of unadulterated strawberries. It was a pretty combination as well as a tasty one. And if there were any serious dieters present, the strawberries alone made a nice alternative dessert. Judging from the relative amounts of leftovers, I'd say the dieters left their diets at home.

On Wining and Dining . . . Consider This

• **Go with your food fantasies.** It's your party. Be as innovative, as elegant, or as laid-back as you please. You can plan thematically, based on location, season, or favorite ethnic foods. Or you can hire a caterer who thinks completely out of the box. Don't feel apologetic about going vegetarian all the way, if that's a matter of principle for you.

• **Don't capitulate to the lowest common denominator.** At least don't capitulate too much. You don't have to resort to a bland menu for fear of offending conservative palates. But don't be fascist, either. Have a familiar item or two on the buffet, alongside the pickled alligator. On the other hand, if all but a few guests are the meat-and-potato types, you can stick to basic fare—exceptionally prepared—with something like an optional pepper sauce on the side.

• **Forgo quantity for quality.** Of course, that's easiest if you're keeping things small. Lobster salad for 20 may be less costly than turkey roll for 200. If you choose less expensive fare, such as chicken, select innovative preparations.

• **Make food integral to the festivities.** Have the cooks do their grilling or flambé-ing publicly, if possible. Or enlist guests in preparing their own tacos, custom-ordering their omelets or selecting their own stir-fry ingredients.

• **Don't buy connoisseur libations for guests who'll be happy with common fare.** Even choosy guests should be too busy socializing to obsess over what's in their glasses. It's okay to select something slightly better than you normally do, in honor of the occasion, especially if the wedding's small. But don't go over the top just to impress.

• **Get a "real" wedding cake—or improvise!** If it's your first wedding, you may want nothing other than tiers of white. Yet nontraditional cakes are neat, too. See what a nontraditional baker has to offer, or ask a baker to execute your own creative whims. How about a giant strawberry shortcake? If your wedding is during Christmas season, why not fruitcake, tiered and frosted in white? For decoration, consider innovative alternatives to the stiff bride-and-groom cake topper. Or create a more personal bride and groom—skiing down the cake, for example, if you're both into that.

~

Your Wedding—The Movie: On Photos and Videos

After the cake is eaten, the guests are gone, the flowers are wilted, and the bills are paid, a wedding lives on in pictures. Documenting my wedding with excellence was of paramount importance to me. If the champagne was half-chilled, the food half-warm, my face half-shiny or the soloist half-flat, I'd get over it. If our photos were less than spectacular, I'd be ill for a lifetime. Even before we finalized the place and date, I began the quest for THE photographer. Everything else could wait.

This would be my One Perfect Thing.

A Wedding Elf told me to track down John. The trouble with most mid-life Wedding Elves is, they're rooted in the past—in realities that may have met the wrecking ball long ago. Back when I was in my teens, John was a highly regarded 20-something photojournalist. When he worked weddings, he didn't do the standard grin-and-pose shots. He did documentary photos—moody, evocative candids in black-and-white. Documentary wedding photography has grown into a popular specialty. I'd like to think that John was among the pioneers.

Fast-forwarding 30 years, it was no surprise to learn that John was now in a prominent position with a major publishing company. This did not deter me from asking—very humbly—if he still did an occasional wedding. I think I added that I sort of knew his sister once. Second question: Could he recommend someone almost as extraordinarily talented as himself? Absolutely! He'd get back to me. The most critical aspect of my wedding was nearly nailed.

For many younger brides, wedding photography isn't a one-day event. Like the engagement period, it's a season.

The season starts with engagement photos—shots of the recently betrothed couple in plainclothes and the full bloom of anticipation. These shots are generally casual in pose, setting and dress.

Once the bride's wedding ensemble is together, it's time for her formal portrait. Hair, makeup, flowers, gown, hairstyle, and bride come together in perfect order for a studio session. For several hours, the bride is bent into unlikely positions. She may be lit as if by moonlight or soft-focused as if an angel. She'll be regal one moment, prayerful the next. The best of these photos will wind up in the newspapers, on Mom and Dad's fireplace mantel and on the newlyweds' brand new buffet.

It's finally the wedding day. But wait: Before the wedding photos come *pre*-wedding photos. Bride and Mom. Bride and Dad. Bride and Mom and Dad. Bride and bridesmaids and flower girl. Bride pins corsage on Mom. Mom and bride look at engagement ring. Separately, the groom is photographed with all his retinue. Best man fixes groom's tie. And so on.

Then come the photos at the ceremony and reception. Let's not forget the intermission between the two, during which the full wedding party goes across town for photos at the botanical garden while the guests get lost between venues, make small talk with strangers, grow hungry and waaaaaiiiitttt.

Mid-lifers don't need all this!! Once they're in the midst of it, I suspect young couples realize they don't need it, either.

Besides wedding photos, all I wanted was an engagement photo. Something that said for eternity: Here's the way we looked at a special time in our lives together. The way we looked "every day," that is. Not in our top-of-the-wedding-cake costumes. I wanted something out-doorsy, in natural light, and a photographer I'd worked with on indus-trial shoots agreed to do the honors. Shelly can make the most self-conscious plant worker look relaxed and natural, so I had no doubt he could do the same for a couple of lovebirds. Future Husband and I put on our jeans and, at Shelly's recommendation, headed to a wooded park at an afternoon hour when the light would be just so.

The results made us remarkably giddy. It wasn't so much because the photos were good, which they were. It was mostly because they were the first photos we'd ever seen of ourselves together.

That was all the posing I intended to do. The portrait studios I later visited never—not rarely, but *never*—get brides over 35. Like long trains and soup-to-nuts gift registries, the bridal portrait is just too "princess."

For our weddings and receptions, all we mid-lifers want to do is get married and party. We typically want photography, but we expect the photographer to do his or her thing with minimal intrusion.

"I can't believe the way some photographers just take control of a wedding," said a woman preparing for her second wedding. "No one should even know the photographer's there."

At my wedding, that could have been the case for real. Despite a number of follow-up calls, I hadn't heard squat from "absolutely" John. The wedding was five weeks away.

"There's a photo studio right here in town," said my mother. "Maybe you should check them out when you're here next weekend."

Now what are the odds I'm going to like an unsung photographer in my parents' backyard? But I'd run out of time to be smug. With buddies Donna and Candy, I paid the studio a visit.

"What is your date?" asked the representative.

May 25th.

"What year?"

If I heard that one more time. . . .

The studio, it turned out, represented several photographers, all of whom had been groomed by the owner and master as specialists in candid wedding shots. We paged through several sample albums from real weddings. All were decent. Two were a striking cut above the rest. Although no photographers were identified on the two albums, the composition, framing and human insight revealed an identical eye. My kind of eye. This photographer would need no direction. And certainly, no candid photographer wants any.

"I'm not sure Gene is available," said the representative, checking the calendar. "Why, yes, it just so happens he is." I booked immediately. And no, I wasn't putting down a nonrefundable deposit for "a photographer." It had to be Gene or nobody. Please. (Don't be smug.)

Candids go only so far. Even mid-lifers need a few posed shots to ensure no VIPs get overlooked. In addition, a decent portrait of the newlyweds shouldn't be left to chance.

"A lot of couples pose for their shots *before* the ceremony," suggested the rep. And have the groom see me in my dress before I come down the aisle?? At other weddings, I've always enjoyed the look of anticipation on the groom's face just before the bride enters. I wanted that tradition, too. And sure enough, the first photo in our album is of the groom waiting at the altar, just shy of *verklempt*.

After the ceremony, while the guests were occupied with their first sips of champagne, we had Gene assemble a few fast shots on the lawn: bride and groom, groom's family and bride's family. A bit later we did the *Godfather* shot: the two of us surrounded by all the Dearly Beloved. It got everyone happily into the act, and it looks great.

Gene was otherwise perfectly unobtrusive, even with an assistant in tow. Yet out of the corner of my eye, I sensed his style and knew the pictures would be good. He vanished from the scene before I had a chance to thank him.

Wedding videos were unheard of when most people of my generation first married. In fact, VCRs and camcorders were unheard of. Today, the wedding video is nearly standard. It's the ultimate wedding document, adding sound and motion to vision. But I wasn't ready for Hollywood—especially for the ceremony. I didn't want *Shelley's Vows: The Movie* any more than I wanted a fairy-tale event. Nor did I want a photographer *and* videographer tripping over one another and killing the solemnity of the moment.

For the reception, on the other hand, I thought video would be neat. Not some professionally shot and edited production, but rather a casual, home-movie approach, warts and all. My mother gave us a video camera as a prewedding gift. During the reception, it was available to anyone who wanted to pick it up and shoot. Even the groom got into the act. Credit for the one and only wart goes to Donna, who was inspired to turn the camera for a vertical shot. Whenever the video is played and that scene comes up, every head in the audience suddenly snaps 90 degrees to the left. Cracks me up every time.

Although mid-lifers are more focused on getting married than staging a show, there are still a few good reasons to put the moment in pictures, be they moving or still. First, getting married is very surreal. Without reminders, I later learned, the bridal brain becomes fuzzy in a hurry about what transpired that day. Entering the age of short-term memory loss doesn't help. Second, you've never looked better and you never will again. Really. So freeze the moment for vanity's sake.

"I've never seen anybody grin so much," said a friend after the wedding. I didn't fathom what she meant until I saw Gene's proofs. They could have been toothpaste ads.

Finally, your visuals are records for the ages—for your own occasional sentimental review, if not for posterity. I was still a newlywed when I came upon Aunt Bern's wedding dress in her apartment. I paused in its honor before stuffing it into the bag for donations. When I came upon her wedding photo, I saved it. Some token of her wedding deserved to be kept by somebody. I hope some stepchild, cousin or family archivist might feel the same way about our album and video one day. If not, well, we will have gotten more than our money's worth from them just the same.

On Photos . . .
Consider This

- **Don't rely on the guests.** If documentation is very important to you, hire someone to take care of it. Don't assign this job to friends. They should attend your wedding as participants, not observers. They may take a lot of pictures or videos and give them to you anyway, and some may be pretty good. But they may not capture every aspect of the event you want.

• **Pick a photographer and videographer who can work with grownups.** Like your other service providers, they should be selected not only for the quality of their work and its appeal to your taste, but also for their style of operation. They should not take over the event. *Yo, everybody, come stand over here.* Nor should they patronize you. *Put your arm on his shoulder; gaze into his eyes.*

• **Let the photographer and videographer be.** Once you've hired people who've won your confidence, leave it to their judgment about what to do. At the outset, however, they'll appreciate having a general sense of your preferences. Let them know who the main family members are. Point out any "required" subjects. Tell them if you're especially interested in children, senior citizens or the gang from the office.

• **Include candid photography.** Candids are great, especially for smaller weddings where most of the guests know each other. The natural camaraderie is conducive to good shots. Even when candids are the rule, let the photographer know if it's okay to ask for the quick attention of a small group.

• **Plan in advance any posed shots you want.** Don't run the risk of forgetting a key portrait. At bare minimum, plan on a portrait of yourself and the groom in your moment of nuptial glory. Stage the posed shots quickly and efficiently, so they barely interrupt the festivities. Having a small wedding party helps. Getting a shot of the whole gang adds to the festivities.

• **Don't obsess about sucking in your tummy or minimizing your laugh lines.** You won't look natural unless you act natural. Leave it to the photographer to minimize your flaws and accentuate the good parts.

• **Do an engagement photo—or whatever you care to call it.** Document *The Way We Were* on an average day. Either hire a pro or enlist a friend who's a pretty good amateur.

Hold the Garter: Reception Rituals

*N*ow the newlyweds will take their first dance as husband and wife. Now the father of the bride will dance with the bride. Now the groom will dance with the mother of the bride. Now the newlyweds would like everyone to join them on the dance floor. . . .

Is this a party or a circus act?

Again, mid-life weddings are more focused on fun than on ritual. We expect the socializing to come naturally. If we happen to like certain traditions, we'll incorporate them. Maybe we'll add an innovative twist; maybe we won't. But we'll avoid any activities that are either too courtly or too juvenile.

We'll also avoid activities that aren't pertinent—like getting showered with rice or birdseed. Most of us are not interested in fertility symbols. If you are, however, a whole lot of birdseed may be in order. (Viagra is not.) Getting showered with symbols of love rather than parenthood is entirely appropriate. As your ceremony ends or as you leave your reception, your guests might enjoy showering you with flower petals, for example.

Do we need a receiving line? *Mother, you remember Joyce from the cheerleading squad, don't you?* No, we do not need this. Our wedding party is probably small, and if the number of guests is small, too, surely we can handle introductions informally as we mingle during the reception. The number of people who are strangers to each other is probably limited in the first place. And if the wedding is large, a receiving line is tedious and foot-unfriendly for both the receivers and the received. You and your groom are better off moving through the crowd and introducing one another to any unknowns.

Yet later, I'd wonder: Did I speak with absolutely everyone? Did everyone meet the groom? Did Susan meet Sam, who graduated from the same school or who works in the same occupation or who also used to live in Boston? I was in a fog. I'll never know.

For sure, we don't need formal introductions of the wedding party by a master of ceremonies. In fact, we don't need a master of ceremonies.

"Heeeeere's Shelley and Gary," or whatever his name was. I was a bridesmaid being introduced with my usher-partner over a loudspeaker by a bubbly catering hall employee. On Gary's arm, I breezed into the ballroom, followed by a spotlight, to thunderous applause. Applause for what? Coming down the aisle of the church without stumbling? Even in my twenties, I found this practice silly. As a mid-lifer, I know why. A wedding, like a marriage, is not a stage play. Fortunately, the bridal couple in this '70's wedding stopped short of floating into the ballroom through a man-made cloud or a flock of a hundred doves.

Toasts are cool. Whether sentimental or funny, they add personality to weddings young and old. And given the significance of the event, a *little* bit of a program within the party seems warranted. Something deserves to be said by somebody. In our case, there was no automatic choice of toastmaster. Traditionally, the best man does the honors. Future Husband didn't have one. Sometimes fathers make toasts. No fatherly voice would be present. I turned to Buddy, our dear and charming family friend.

Elaine and her groom each invited an age-peer friend to deliver their wedding toasts. That was nicely democratic. Each toast paid loving homage to what was special about the bride or the groom and why they deserved this happiness.

Buddy embraced his responsibility with fervor. He needed a sense of direction, however, and quite rightly he asked me for it. I was still canvassing the region for a violinist, trying to schedule a meeting with the caterer and starting to worry that I wouldn't have a photographer. Now I had yet another thing to do! Delegation doesn't make a task disappear, and I hadn't a clue about what the toastmaster should say. Buddy helped by probing about my courtship with Future Husband. He took matters into his own hands from there.

As everyone gathered in a circle, champagne in hand, Buddy delivered his toast with the help of a cheat sheet cleverly taped to the back of his glass. The toast was lighthearted yet eloquent. That's my hazy recollection; I've forgotten every word.

When the toast was done, I shared remarks of my own. "Remarks" may be too strong a word. On behalf of my groom and myself, I had planned to set the tone for the reception. I wanted to invite everyone to share a celebration of romance, and not just ours. I wanted couples to celebrate their own romance. I wanted singles to recall and renew the promise of it. Though I'd been thinking these thoughts for weeks, I hadn't prepared so much as a note. I winged it. If memory serves, I mumbled something fairly inarticulate.

Some time after the wedding, my mother told me she'd intended to ask Buddy to welcome any other guests to make comments after his toast was done. She read my mind. That would have been nice. Some time even later, I stumbled upon some notes she'd written for her own remarks. My somewhat stage-shy mother had prepared to rise to the occasion. Both of us probably would have gotten quiver-lipped.

Having the groom publicly remove your garter and toss it to a bunch of guys is antiquated and sexist. But if you're willing to extinguish the fire in your brassiere for a moment, it can provide a lot of laughs, even in a mature, mid-life way. I chose to skip this ritual, however.

I also chose not to toss my bouquet. In the unlikely event that any of my single female friends were desperate to marry, I didn't want them making inelegant spectacles of themselves. Nor did I like the idea of female competition. Then again, I recall a wedding where, amid the giddy young ladies positioning themselves in the outfield, a 50-something woman stood tall and patiently waited for the toss of the bouquet. She looked amazingly dignified.

What I meant to do, toward the end of the reception, was to present each female friend, married or single, with a single flower from my bouquet. The flower would represent my wish for each friend's happiness in love in whatever individual way was right. It would symbolize my own reawakened faith. I discovered, unfortunately, there was no neat way to pluck one flower at a time from the bouquet. I intended to ask someone to help me figure it out, but—you know the refrain—I forgot.

Where was the emcee when I needed him? *The bride will now dismember her bouquet. . . .*

Wedding guests—especially those who least know the others—enjoy opportunities to engage in something, and our backyard setting seemed to beg for recreation. We set up a croquet set, and sure enough, several people got into it, including the bride. I have a sentimental shadow of a grass stain on one shoe to this day. Others just enjoyed watching. A couple of boys found a ball from I-don't-know-where and got into a game of catch.

There was neither a dance floor nor any specific expectation of dancing. However, when the music and spirit moved us, my groom and I grabbed each other for a couple of impromptu dances on the patio. Our guests watched and smiled, but I was disappointed that no one joined us. Perhaps they needed specific information: *This is an informal wedding. Please do your thing.* I thought they'd get this message on their own, but maybe I expected too much.

"With our *hands*?"

The ceremonial cutting of the cake sounded nice to Future Husband, as I explained it in advance. But he was less enthusiastic about the "raw American" follow-up of feeding one another with bare fingers. He feeds himself even hamburgers and pizza with knife and fork. Yet he indulged me in the cake thing, and in the end, I think it amused him. Over the years, some younger couples have taken the tradition to mud pit extremes, mashing cake all over one another's faces. Mid-life couples simply don't do this. We may be silly enough to stuff a slightly oversized chunk or lick our partner's fingers, but we don't get gooey beyond the lip line or second knuckle.

Tess and her husband went to the other extreme and used forks.

It's an old-fashioned tradition for the newlyweds to be first to leave, so the guests can give them a rousing send-off. When the newlyweds are also the hosts, however, this practice seems odd, if not inappropriate. We were the last to leave, which I found a bit quiet and lonely. In my "trousseau," a favorite dress from the closet, I departed with my new husband in my car, which was refreshingly free of spray paint, balloons and the like. I suppose clattering cans are a thing of the past.

Months later, as we arrived at a favorite lunch spot, we saw a minivan in the parking lot with *Just Married* and a bunch of hearts sprayed all over the windows. Out of the restaurant came a gray-haired couple who got in this vehicle and drove away. Those wild and crazy kids! That would have been a bit much for me. But I wish I'd had maybe a single balloon or flag on the radio antenna, telling the world about the greatest thing I'd ever done.

On Reception Rituals . . .
Consider This

• **Put a twist on familiar rituals.** Show your innovative side. Remove *his* garter, for example, and toss it to your rowdy female friends.

• **Avoid courtly and stagy rituals.** The receiving line is unnecessary. In its place, however, you'll need to make a conscious effort to make introductions. Keep at least a mental list of whom you most want to meet whom. Even at a small gathering, it's easy to become distracted and forget.

• **Incorporate religious or ethnic traditions as you wish.**

• **Include toasts, roasts or tributes.** They're inevitably a hit. In advance, you and your groom can request remarks from one special person or a few. Consider a mix of generations—peers, elders, teenage children. In advance or impromptu, you can invite anyone to speak up. If it's a small wedding, everyone knows you or your groom pretty well. Some have known you many years. During your adulthood alone, they may have witnessed a transformation or two. Giving guests a theme sometimes helps, such as: *The funniest / sweetest / dumbest thing I've ever known the groom / bride to do is*_____.

• **Address the crowd yourself.** In addition to thanking the guests for coming, briefly say something about what the marital kickoff and gathering of loved ones means to you. You can do the talking yourself, leave it to your groom or do it together.

• **Enlist an assistant host.** While you're running your mouth or simply floating in the clouds, she can help introduce people to one another, entertain bored children or ensure people know their way back home. Ask a friend or relative, not a hired hand, to take care of these personal activities.

• **Draw out the crowd.** Even though you expect the reception to be a natural party, your guests might not naturally get the point. Specifically invite them to dance or engage in other activities. If you're having a huge affair, an engaging emcee or band leader may be just the ticket. Look for a truly refreshing personality as opposed to the average lounge lizard.

• **Dance with the special men in your life.** You don't need your every dancing move announced. Yet it's still nice to have an impromptu dance with your groom, father, son, father-in-law, anyone you please. Don't worry about the order of people. No choice of dance partner is inappropriate. Nor do you have to wait for a man to do the inviting. Of course, all of the above goes for your groom and his women, too.

• **Go ahead and have fun with the cake cutting.** If you don't need to take a shower afterward, you've acted your age.

• **Leave the reception whenever it suits you.** You can leave first, last or somewhere in the middle. If you're not last, make sure an assistant host remains to see to everyone's comfort until the end.

• **Somebody: Please bestow individual flowers from your bouquet on your women friends.** I need this vicarious experience.

Oh, No, More Stuff: Managing Gifts

"**G**et them a waffle iron," my father used to advise my mother before she went shopping for a wedding gift. "Every man should be able to have hot waffles on Sunday mornings."

I'm dead certain he didn't intend for the men to prepare the waffles themselves. But the point was, and is, gifts are the traditional way to help newlyweds feather their first nests as well as begin the acquisition of a lifetime of treasures.

"Where are you registered?" a friend asked Elaine.

Nowhere.

"No, *you* are going to be registered," countered the friend. Elaine quickly saw the light: Who needs the hassle of returning, let alone keeping, gifts you don't like, and then having to explain? And why put the burden of decision-making on friends? They're busy people, too, with better things to do than wondering what you'd like and where to find it.

For young brides, registering for gifts can be like a grownup visit to Santa Claus—a joyful opportunity to wish for a bounty of stuff. For some mid-lifers, the gift thing is more uncomfortable. It seems inappropriate for us to expect help with "starting our lives." Besides, we've already got stuff in spades. And it's keeper stuff: Long ago, we replaced our complete set of free-with-a-fill-up glasses and the flatware we "borrowed" from the college cafeteria. Actually, I still have this one fork. . . .

It was our generation of single women that chucked the notion of the temporary bachelor household. By age 30 or so, it dawned on us to be good to ourselves *now*. If we were making a living, we didn't have to postpone having things we wanted for the long term. We could have serious pots and pans. We could have thick, thirsty towels. We didn't have to wait for a husband to have a "real" home.

So, as a bride, you bring to the table—and to the linen closet and kitchen cabinet—stuff that's in perfectly good shape and that you value. Unless you've been cohabitating, the groom has separate stuff of his own. That amounts to stuff times two. If either of you has received the spoils of a previous marriage, wedding gifts included, that more or less equals stuff times two, squared. Now your friends and loved ones want to shower you with yet more stuff. You're not ungrateful, but . . . good grief!

To come up with gift ideas, couples need to take at least a general inventory and figure out where the gaps in stuff are. Here's the good news: There's inevitably a gap or two. Future Husband and I had duplicate sets of everyday everything—plates, toasters, coffee makers. We were beginning to collect good porcelain tableware, but they were hard-to-find antiques. Asking guests to find the missing puzzle pieces would be punitive. Besides, scouring flea markets and estate sales was a favorite hobby, and we wanted to keep it up. But aha! What we needed, and what guests could readily find, was some new crystal stemware. On to the registry.

Bridal registries don't have a lot of customers over 40, but they get more these days than ever.

"Oh, yes, they come in. I've *seen* them!" whispered a salesperson in a department store, as if confiding a sighting of Elvis.

I didn't want to register, but everyone's asking. That's the typical line of the mid-life customer, according to the store's registry manager. Hello, Elaine.

You're more likely to register if it's your first wedding or the groom's. After all, an entitlement has been earned, so to speak, so you cash it in. Some mid-lifers fill in china or silver patterns they already have. "They often ask *Does this Lenox pattern still exist?*" says the manager. In some cases, their patterns are inherited. "They're at that age."

Once again, Mom's out of the selection process, although one registry manager recalled a 40-something first-time bride who selected gifts with the 80-something parents of the *groom*. "They had so much fun!" More likely, it's you and the groom registering together, and your groom is fully engaged in the selection of monograms and serving dishes.

Our stemware took little time to register. We'd settled on manufacturer, pattern, pieces and numbers long before going to the store. More often than younger brides, we arrive at a bridal registry with at least a general idea of what we want. And with some possessions already established, we don't register for the whole enchilada.

"A lot of our mid-life customers have smaller weddings, even if it's their first," says a manager. "Instead of creating a three-page list, they usually focus on one thing."

The look you're after is apt to be more classic than trendy. But before you consider style, you'll look for quality and durability. "Older couples ask the kinds of questions that mothers of younger couples usually ask," says the manager. Practicality is also key: You're not likely to list a strictly decorative item such as a vase. Nor will you list a toothpick holder, crumb sweeper, shrimp forks, or any other odd pieces you know darn well you'll never use.

Why do we know this? Because we've been entertaining for a lot of years, be it every week or every blue moon. Unless you're hosting a picnic, the days of paper plates and plastic cups are history. Now you serve with your good things.

Young newlyweds will proudly display their new treasures under lights in their new china cabinets. You, however, will frequently take your treasures *out* of the cabinet and use them—even if it's just for Sunday dinner for two.

So much for the fancy goods. A bridal registry should include some alternatives for your friends' consideration. Since Future Husband and I both enjoy cooking, we thumbed through the catalog of a kitchen specialty store and made a list of cool things that caught our imagination—an olive oil can, monogrammed aprons, a pasta maker, a grill for small veggies. We needed none of these things, but we knew if we had them, we'd use them.

"How about some wind chimes?" Elaine suggested off the top of her head to a friend in need of a gift suggestion. The wind chimes were such a hit with Elaine and her husband that they now buy a new set of chimes on every anniversary. I hope their neighbors like wind chimes, too.

Besides wind chimes, there are a host of nontraditional gifts you can register for if the cup, saucer, and linen thing is too old-fashioned for the aging rebel in you. You can register artwork, for example, or hardware and tools. If you're landscaping a new home, shrubs and trees can be listed. Many retailers you'd hardly expect are offering bridal registries, and many that don't will be glad to create one for you.

Honeymoon registries are growing popular, especially with second-timers. "We break the gifts down into breakfast-in-bed, for example, or scuba diving lessons," says a travel agent who specializes in honeymoons.

If you still feel ridiculous having people furnish your "start" in life, you could say "no gifts, please." However, that's kind of party pooperish when your loved ones want to do *something*. Better to suggest alternative ways they can satisfy their generous spirit. You can "list" your favorite charities, for example. This practice unfortunately suggests funerals more than weddings. However, the giving will please you and the charities, too.

Note that the "no gift" approach can backfire. One Christmas season when I was in my twenties, I got fed up with the material frenzy of the holiday. I recommended to my family that we give each other no gifts that year and, in so doing, better appreciate the true meaning of Yuletide. They said okay. Christmas morning, they had gifts for me; I had none for them. "We couldn't help but do a little something. . . ."

So take heed: Your friends may give to charity *and* to you, and what you get, you may not want. But that's a small price to pay for love.

The day after our wedding, Husband and I bashfully eyeballed and fingered the bounty that Mom had spread all over her guest-room bed. It was like Christmas morning and then some. Having gifts shipped directly to our own home was far more efficient, but not nearly as touching as this array of treasures among tissue paper, ribbons, and sentimental cards. Thanks to our registries, the element of surprise was mostly missing, but so was the element of dismay.

Ironically, one of our favorite gifts—a hand-painted plate by a favorite porcelain maker—was a surprise. The prize for most sentimental gifts went to Husband's aunts for a few personal keepsakes—more surprises. Neither did we expect cash and checks, the ultimate symbols of starting life from scratch. With them, we opened our first joint bank account. It was an oddly romantic event.

Perhaps I've bad-mouthed surprise gifts too harshly.

On Managing Gifts . . . Consider This

- **Register or regret it.**

- **Figure out the gaps in what you need or want.** Start by taking a general inventory of the things you and your groom have *and* want to keep.

- **Shop through stores or catalogs.** With your groom, negotiate and narrow down your selections before seeing the registrar to make a list.

- **Register someplace convenient.** Since friends and family may be far-flung, find a registry that's almost everywhere nationwide or available on the World Wide Web.

- **Make sure you both agree to keeping your pattern or his.** Filling out an existing pattern is fine, so long as that's what you both want for your future lives *together*. If the pattern is from your previous marriage, make sure he can truly accept your ex's ex-plates.

• **Give your guests options.** Even if you need to list only flatware, guests may feel a loss of individual expression if they're buying the same thing everyone else is buying. Think of alternatives as well as a range of prices.

• **Include nontraditional gifts.** If an aging rebel lives within, register for—or simply suggest—an azalea, a ratchet set, a bird feeder, a honeymoon. Many friends will get a kick out of the change of pace. And if you're a second-timer, maybe some of these friends filled your cupboard with china, flatware and other household basics once before. Isn't it a bit bold to expect them to set you up "for life" all over again?

• **In lieu of gifts, request charitable donations.** If you just don't want gifts, or if you prefer to steer generosity in a needier direction, invite friends to give donations to a favorite charity— maybe one of yours and one of his. Give people more than one option, in case they can't get excited about saving the slug.

• **Don't worry about surprise gifts.** You've invited your close friends, not your father's accountant. They probably know your tastes fairly well.

At Last

In younger days, I hypothetically imagined waking up on my wedding day, getting smacked in the head by reality and bailing out. Instead, my reality this morning is no different than it has been for days, weeks and months in advance. Everything is right as rain.

Speaking of which, there hasn't been any rain all week. The month of May has been sunnier, bluer and warmer than usual. The forecast called for more of the same, but surely the odds were lousy. Plan B is to hold the wedding in the living room. I don't like Plan B, and I've been ignoring it assiduously. To be wed in the womb of nature would not only be romantic and pretty; it seems spiritually important.

Our luck holds out, in spades.

I had a solid night's sleep, guaranteed perhaps by a Wedding Eve on wheels. It was the previous night that I slept poorly, reviewing the mental checklist of wedding trivia. By the morning of the Big Mo, the only thing left to do is hope and trust: I hope Donna and Sandy, my directors, can follow my script. I hope the musicians can find their way to the house. I hope Calvin the minister will arrive early enough to give us a clear idea of what we're supposed to do. Bottom line is, I trust that none of the above matters overwhelmingly. If something isn't perfect, we'll punt.

"Perfection is imperfection," Barbra Streisand told *In Style*, explaining her wedding day attitude. That's a stretch, Barbra, but I like it.

I take a premarital run to get into my private space. I meet a party rental truck on the road and realize, hey, that's *my* party rental truck. My steps are momentarily lighter for it. On the way back, I meet the hill that often mocks me, enticing me to quit and walk the final paces up to the crest. Not today, hill. I am Bride; hear me roar. My run summons no heavy contemplation. No absorption into my past, future or the passage in between. I just feel good in the moment.

By the time I return home—one's childhood house is forever "home"—Nearly Husband is there in shorts and T-shirt, unfolding chairs in the yard. Having him see me before the wedding is an old taboo I couldn't care less about. Plus I'm wearing Spandex and sweat, not my dress. Two days earlier, we analyzed the position of the sun at precisely 4:00 p.m. Now we carefully arrange chairs so none of the Dearly Beloved will have to squint. We disagree on strategy, just like real married people.

Last chance to conjure the fairy godmother and her wand: I shower, shampoo, condition, exfoliate and moisturize. I've forgotten the cucumber slices for my eyes, but a mere two months of good behavior have actually left my face unblemished and smooth. As I look in the mirror, something else is evident. I'm, well, radiant. Even for midlifers, this bridal myth seems to hold true.

Three hours vanish. It's lift-off minus 60 minutes, and Calvin has just finished briefing us on the ceremony and getting signatures on the license from us and our witnesses. I imagine Nearly Stepson's signature's signature as approval, which is nice. I imagine Mom's signature as permission, which is funny.

Now Calvin is keeping Nearly Husband occupied and almost relaxed with chitchat in the living room while the florist and caterer scurry about doing their thing. I think. I'm holed up in my childhood bedroom, not certain of what's going on beyond the door. I'm an improbable princess in an ivory tower. In the driveway outside the window, God

Brother Scott postures in aviator sunglasses, smooth as the Secret Service, waiting for the first sign of wedding traffic to direct.

I devote maybe five minutes instead of the usual three to my makeup. My designated Big Mo underwear is in the laundry room, separated from me by two flights of stairs and various people. I take Queen Margaret's attitude: At Buckingham Palace on Princess Elizabeth's wedding day, the bride's tiara broke as it was placed on her head. Said cool Margaret: "Well, there's certainly more than one tiara around here."

Bridesmaid Heather enters my tower, pretty in long pink lace. Donna and Sandy enter to go over the script and otherwise hover. Donna begins her trademark wringing of hands, threatening my inner peace. I shoo them out.

Stepping into the dress, I realize one fabric flower still sits on the tail bone. In my ambivalence, I had the seamstress leave on one flower out of three, which I could snip off later if I wanted. Now I fear I look like a bunny, and I want a second opinion from my mother. I can faintly detect her voice, among others, elsewhere in the house. Maybe she's busy helping get my father dressed. Maybe she's getting dressed herself. Maybe she's talking with the caterer. All I know is: I want my Mommy, and she's left me to my own grownup care.

"Do you think your mother has a slip I can borrow?"

What? Donna is back in my tower, because her husband has advised her that her dress is translucent in the sunshine. She's mortified, not because of the dress, but because her husband has talked her into seeking rescue from the bride, who might have better things to do at lift-off minus 20. Embarrassment for her; comic relief for me.

Guests are mingling in the living room when they should be on the patio. How were they to know? What I need is a runner. *Tell Nearly Husband to tell the others. . . .* Thanks to Donna and Sandy, they all move to their seats on the lawn at the appointed hour.

Jesu, Joy of Man's Desiring. . . .

It's just me and Heather in the tower now, and her cue is fast approaching. I fiddle with my headpiece and lift the bodice of my dress onto my shoulders. *I'm ready as I'm going to get for my closeup, Mr. DeMille.*

"Don't you want to take off your bra?" asks Heather. I flip around in front of the mirror. The dress is backless, and I've forgotten to ditch the brassiere at the last moment. Bridal distraction and short-term memory loss are a dangerous mix. Heather gets my vote for Bridesmaid of the Year.

I approach the top of the steps and watch Heather glide out the door (to the wrong music). Nicola catches my eye. Our soloist is brilliant not only in voice but also in a resplendent African-inspired dress and head wrap. I'm impressed even as she upstages me. I see the crowd outside—and I do mean "crowd." Forty-eight people look like 400. The sun points squarely in half their eyes. A whole front row of seats is empty. My Almost In-Laws have no idea those seats are theirs.

Lohengrin will start thumping at any moment, and—oh, shoot—the multitudes are going to stand and turn my way, aren't they? I make my way down the steps. The third step probably didn't creak when I made that first bridal descent at age five. I didn't creak then either, and I don't intend to for many years to come.

PART THREE

With This Ring, I Thee Blend into the Rest of My Life Somehow

Getting the Hang of It

F ive months into marriage, it's time for a new driver's license, and
I'm as thrilled as an eighth-grader. I've had a few driver's licenses
in 30 years, but this will be the first license—the first *anything*—in my
new name.

A week later, I'm about to board a plane.

"May I see a photo ID?" asks the agent. Uh-oh. My only photo ID
is the new driver's license, and my ticket's in my other name—my
business name. The agent lets me get by with a photo-less department
store charge card.

I promptly got hold of my travel agent. "From now on, you've got
to issue my tickets in my married name!"

"You won't get mileage credit," she advised, "unless you change
your name on your frequent flyer accounts, too." That was just the first
domino. I would also have to rename myself on the credit cards that
bestow mileage credit. I'd have to change my passport, too. I waited
for a long, travel-free window of opportunity to put all my accounts in
synch. A simple phone call or click of the mouse won't cut it with most

institutions. One must send letters, marriage licenses, notarized forms and such.

Today, there isn't one piece of identification in my wallet bearing my lifetime name. I'd never anticipated that. It's sort of sad.

Outside the wallet, I make full use of two separate surnames, as planned. That's proved gratifying. I'm whichever self I care to be for a given purpose. It's a system not without problems, however.

"Moore?? Who's that?" says Husband when a message or piece of mail arrives in my original name. This is the same Husband who said premaritally that my choice of name made no difference to him. It's mock outrage, but there's a detectable smidgen of sensitivity. Mid-life husbands aren't quite as indifferent to the "other name" as they'd like to be.

When I show up at the security desk at the office of a certain client, I announce my business name. When I show up at the same office to visit Husband, who happens to work there, I announce my married name. In either case, I try to get there before 3 P.M., when the *smart* security guard goes off duty. I baffle the heck out of the relief guy. Certainly, I could give the guards a break and use my business name consistently. But frankly, I forget. When the purpose is personal, my personal name tends to come out of my mouth. And once you identify yourself one way, you sound kind of foolish changing your mind.

Other clients still know me by one name only. There's been no confusion, not counting the time a client first sent me on a trip. "I'll make your reservations," said the secretary.

"Thanks." Next day: "Wait! You've got to use another name." *All this time, see, I've been a fraud.*

Whichever name I call myself rings false even to me. The last place anyone wants to look like a fraud is the bank. Whenever I stand in line to deposit a business-name check into my personal-name account, I pray not to get the anal-retentive teller.

So much for getting everyone else acquainted with the new you. Besides your name, by the way, nothing much is fundamentally new about you. Your foremost challenge is to get your same, old autonomous self integrated into partnership on a full-time, iron-clad basis.

This is what you've hungered for most—not the engagement, not the wedding, not the honeymoon, but this marriage. Are you ready? Absolutely. Will it be a piece of cake? Some changes will indeed be as welcome as a warm Jacuzzi. As for the rest, well. . . .

Start up the roller coaster.

We Don't Need Smoked Duck: Living Mutually

"This silk blouse should be washed in cold water, gentle cycle, mild soap; no-heat cycle in dryer, ten minutes; hang to dry."

I turn my back fast, lest I see my blouse go into the heavy-duty cycle with bleach. Sure, I could do my own laundry all the time, and he could do his. But this is a marriage, and I really want to be a team player. I'm also grateful that Husband needs no awareness training about couple's work versus women's work. After several months, I've come to trust that my blouse and everything else will come out of the wash fine—because he'll secretly do it my way or because his way is really as good. I still try not to watch.

Before marriage, smart couples of all ages make sure they're generally on the same page about the big things—values, goals, lifestyle, tastes, and the way we process information. But little differences will pop up in spades. You may be the most agreeable, conciliatory person on the planet. However, it's been a long time, or maybe forever, since you've had to reconcile basic matters of lifestyle and home.

Food! I'm into fish, chicken, and abundant green stuff. His four major food groups are cholesterol, coffee, chocolate, and peanuts. As his guest, I got accustomed to the occasional grilled steak. Won't kill me, I rationalized. But now we live together. Do we cook and eat two separate meals? No, that wouldn't be "family."

Air! Maybe you can't sleep comfortably unless a window is cracked open. However, he likes the window closed. Maybe you like to keep the house lights dim; maybe he prefers all lights ablaze. Maybe you'd like classic rock on the radio alarm, while he expects you to bounce out of bed to Brahms.

On issues of religion and politics, you can ultimately agree to disagree. But issues of dinner, windows, radio alarms and the like must be resolved.

When you and your partner lived independently, issues like these were no big deal in small doses. You could compromise when you were together; do your own thing when you were apart. Now you're together 24-7. Constant reconciliation and compromise won't drive you to divorce court, but it'll leave some of you dumfounded.

Fortunately, mid-lifers are still capable of learning. I've learned that it's quite nice to awaken to a symphony. He's learned that while it takes just half an hour to grill chicken legs, it takes a full hour to grill them *well.*

When learning fails, as it often does, many issues can be resolved through innovation. Husband and I brew coffee the way *he* likes it— caustic enough to strip paint. With a splash of hot water, it's perfect for me. I absently follow this routine even when he's out of town.

When innovation fails, as it often does, only one solution remains: surrender. Marriage joins wills and egos as well as hearts. You and your husband may be equally accustomed to being your own monarch. Now it's best if you rotate places on the throne. Of course, no one should do all the surrendering all the time. If one of you is always the unhappy camper, soon both of you will be. So sometimes I give Husband the tie-breaking vote on what movie to rent or whether to buy that beautiful but expensive painting. Sometimes he gives the vote to me.

Sounds basic, doesn't it? The longer you've been a solo act, the less basic this principle is in practice. Some of you may tend to a polar extreme—as a natural tyrant or a natural doormat. Neither role does a partnership justice. You'd better moderate, and fast. As an only child and then a single adult, I was rarely forced to stick to my guns. I *had* all the guns. Now I feel guilty if I get my way, and I feel gutless if I don't. If I'd grown up with siblings, I'd be more confident that people can disagree—even vehemently—and be best friends again by morning.

Every blue moon, I inadvertently push his hot button, or he pushes mine: I spotted a beautiful smoked duck at the deli one day. "Want to try it?" I asked.

"No, we don't need any smoked duck."

We?? Don't arrive at too many "joint" conclusions independently, buster.

I'm the stereotypical wife! The one that's parodied in sitcoms, cartoons, and greeting cards for the art of the "honey-do." It's hardly my deliberate role, and I hope I don't play it to distraction. On the other hand, I'm fascinated at my apparent membership in the universal sisterhood of wives. Yesterday, I was my own woman. Today, I am my own woman *and* the proverbial Woman of the House. Pretty neat. On our second weekend of living together in matrimony, I convinced Husband to clean out the garage. No lie. I even directed the effort. *That's* over the top, but at least I assisted in the execution. Husband isn't enamored of honey-do's, but he understands they go along with the gold ring. He's a seasoned second-timer. Good thing one of us is.

While conference and consensus are important, don't rule out the executive decision. It's often expedient; occasionally it's necessary. *I was too busy to cook; we're ordering a pizza.* Or *I invited my niece to stay with us this weekend.* You must choose your executive decisions carefully, of course. Once you've gotten a handle on what your partner cares about most and least, it's not so difficult.

I'm relieved I'm not of my mother's generation. Throughout her marriage, she kept accounts, paid the bills, called the plumber, fought City Hall, and otherwise managed the household. Yet she never made a key decision about any of it. Fix the boiler or replace it? Pay down on the mortgage or invest in something else? Mom may have expressed an opinion, but my father always made the call. As his illness progressed, Mom had to become the household decider. It was one of the toughest marital adjustments she ever faced.

Today Husband and I laugh about the smoked duck. Now we've graduated to building a house together—a project of endless decisions. Behind our property is a house built by a couple who put it on the market a year later. "They're divorcing," the real estate agent confided to me. This was long before I met Husband. At the time, I could not fathom how a couple could build a house one moment and divorce the next.

Now I can. Husband and I have debated nearly every detail down to the towel bars. We nearly went to the mat over the selection of flooring. Thank goodness, our partnership is as solid as our chosen wood. But I'm not saying who made the final choice.

On Living Mutually . . . Consider This

• **Commit to team consensus, even if you don't fully get it yet.**

• **When you disagree, choose from several options:** Listen, learn, and change your mind. Speak with reason and change *his* mind. Innovate. Compromise. Surrender. Take charge.

• **Change your ways.** Are you a dictator? A wimp? Then you may have a clue to the cause or effect of your long-time solo status. Work on moderating your behavior now, for the good of your marriage and your personal peace of mind. Learn to be forthright *and* diplomatic. It's not easy to change in mid-life, but make a concerted effort anyway.

• **Don't rule out executive decision-making.** Sometimes it's the most practical thing to do.

• **Take advantage of opportunities for autonomy.** Continue to make your own decisions in matters that are strictly personal, such as clothing, hairstyle, fitness, car, for example. Consider his opinions, but do your own thing. Go with a girlfriend to that "chick flick" you want to see. Have sprouts or peanut butter for dinner—whatever you crave that he doesn't—if and when he goes out of town.

• **Keep levity in your decision-making sessions.** Should the atmosphere get testy, make up as quickly as possible afterward.

• **Compartmentalize decisions.** This may be necessary if joint decisions become nearly impossible. You can make all the financial decisions, for example, while he makes all the household decisions. This strategy isn't as ideal as full integration. But sometimes it's the only way to keep peace.

• **Delegate gently.** So what if "honey-do's" are a stereotype? They're a natural part of a working partnership. Be selective. Don't overdo it. Respect any delegation you get in return.

~

Our Tax Refund: Your Money

"I'm not wealthy, but I make a salary that's more than adequate, and I've got a few investments, including the house," said Future Husband. "I just wanted you to know."

What was that about? A long moment passed before it dawned on me that Future Husband was presenting his credentials. This occurred way back, long before we'd started discussing our future, let alone the "m" word. Already he was giving me his qualifications. It was quaint, and it was antiquated. As antiquated as his discomfort when I picked up the check on our third date. I advised him to get over it. He did.

Men are their fathers' sons, and being the breadwinner was still a husband's duty when mid-life men were in their formative years. The breadwinner mind-set beats the deadbeat mind-set by a knockout. Nonetheless, it presumes that a woman must be supported, and that's a bit grating to the woman who has pulled her own weight all her adult life. In marriage, most of us are prepared and willing to be interdependent.

So did I come back at him with my own credentials? Get outta here! My financial profile wasn't his business any more than his was mine.

Eventually these truths would change. But I wasn't prepared to open up then and there. Equality and privacy—two of the strongest tenets of independent womanhood—don't always jibe.

"Here's the ATM card, checkbook, and credit card," said Husband after we'd wed.

I'd never put my hands in anyone else's pocket before, and I wasn't comfortable doing it now.

"It's not *my* money; it's *our* money," Husband tried to explain. As the previously married partner, he gets this. He says things like "I was thinking about paying off the car loan." A long moment passes before I realize: He's waiting for my opinion! Gosh, I don't know. It's his car and his debt. Okay, now it's our car, our debt, but I still feel like I'm butting in.

What's his is mine, and vice versa—a concept more easily embraced in principle than in the gut. That's true for all newlyweds and especially true for mid-lifers who are longtime independents. It's not that you don't trust your partner. It's just that the notion of combining, coordinating or comanaging money is confusing and awkward.

What's more, you each have extremely ingrained ideas, or at least habits, when it comes to the ways you spend, save, invest, lend, borrow, contribute, and monitor money. In assessing your partner's character and values early on, you had the wisdom to ensure that his money habits were compatible with your own. But those habits will never be identical.

Now what? Should you commingle finances? Should you maintain separate pots? Should you share expenses equally? Or should you concoct a formula based on income or assets? Some couples settle these details in their prenups. Other couples do it with a handshake.

Thus far, Husband and I have maintained our respective pots as separate parts of one whole. Husband is by far the better monitor, regularly updating every account, investment, income and expense in a software program and proudly generating financial profiles with colorful graphs and pie charts. I, on the other hand, peek at incoming statements just long enough to ensure nothing scary has happened, then throw them in the file. At any given moment, I have no idea where my whole pot stands.

We share information about the status of our respective pots, and occasionally we offer "advice."

"Why don't you put some of that extra monthly income toward paying down the debt on the house?" I'll ask. He'll ask, "Do you still have a big chunk of money in a savings account earning 2 percent?" Like many men, he believes savings accounts are for chumps. Sometimes we take one another's advice; sometimes we don't. And that's okay, because we're each confident that the other won't do anything totally foolish with his or her part of the whole.

For most mid-lifers, retirement is a foremost financial goal. And we can't call this goal "long-term" any more. Now, it's mid-term and rushing toward us faster every day. I pulled Husband, grumbling all the way, into a financial-planning seminar—one of those shock treatment sessions where they threaten that unless you've socked away a trillion dollars by age 50, you face an old age in the gutter. Husband, of course, didn't need any such seminar. After all, he's Man; knows all. But the seminar reassured both of us that we weren't handling our money too shabbily. We were also reminded of the minor sins we continue to commit. I got to elbow Husband once or twice during the talk. He got to elbow me.

Husband paid for darn near everything at the start of the marriage, which I didn't much like. He reasoned: "You quit your job to be with me, you're starting a business, and you're still paying a mortgage on your unsold apartment." Plus he really can't get past being the provider; I know it. But my circumstances rendered my cries of equality toothless. So I timidly began using his credit card for groceries and other household essentials. Before long, I could whip it out without a second thought. Amazing.

I still don't touch the ATM card, however. And Husband doesn't have my ATM card, credit card, checkbook or anything else.

I find ways of making my contribution. I pay the phone bills. I make most of our travel arrangements, so I quietly pay for them, too. Above all, I demand responsibility for my personal expenses—clothes, hair, car, cat. On one occasion *before* we married, I all but caused a scene at a boutique when Future Husband paid for a dress. And whatever portion of our joint tax refund is "mine" goes into the pot he uses to pay most of our bills.

Taxes! Now there's a conundrum. For most couples, to be "married filing jointly" versus "married filing separately" reduces the overall tax bite and thus makes the most sense. But that's where the sense ends. What portion of your refund represents *your* refund? What portion of taxes owed represents your debt? For perhaps your entire working life, you've played "Beat the IRS" on your own. Now your income, deductions, and estimated or withheld taxes are blended beyond distinction with someone else's. Your tax rate may have jumped, too. Suddenly, you no longer know your individual score, and it's frustrating.

Jeanne and her husband file separately, fully mindful of their combined financial loss. According to my accountant, they're not alone. I'm hardly surprised—especially for couples who've chosen to keep all money matters separate. That first tax year of our marriage, I asked our accountant to do the separate math for the heck of it. Husband and I weren't planning to divvy up the refund; I just wanted to know my score.

"Actually," reported the accountant, "you would have paid the least amount of taxes if you'd stayed single." Very interesting. But not nearly as interesting as my marriage.

On Money . . .
Consider This

• **Decide whether to mingle your money or keep it separate.** It's a matter of comfort level as well as convenience. Many couples do a bit of both. The optional approach applies to postmarriage money only. Assets you acquired prior to marriage are best kept in your own name. (See "That Other Marriage Contract.")

• **Think about sharing expenses according to relative incomes.** Exclude individual responsibilities, such as alimony, college tuition, or prior debt. Use incoming funds before spending funds that earn more funds. If and when relative incomes change substantially—due to a pay raise or a layoff, for example—adjust the sharing of the load.

• **Manage some of your money separately, if you wish.** Marriage is about enjoying things together, money included. Still, you may wish to keep full control of some or all of your own stash. You may have some independent financial objectives, such as a trust fund for your family. Your money management style may be tighter or wackier than his. You may simply be uncomfortable having his hand in your funds, and vice versa. You may also wish to hedge the overall portfolio: If you think he handles money too conservatively, invest more of your own on the wild side.

• **Discuss your financial moves with one another.** Even if you're managing money separately, seek a second opinion from your partner. Give feedback to him, too. At the very least, keep one another abreast of what you're doing. Make sure you're staying on the right course toward your joint goals. Learn from one another's better habits.

• **Share ATM and credit cards if and when you're ready.** Readiness is yet another matter of comfort plus convenience. The sharing can begin later rather than sooner, if you need time to adjust to the idea. Before putting both names on investment or bank accounts, understand the consequences for your estate plan. (See "That Other Marriage Contract.")

• **Know where the books are.** If you're managing money separately, still be familiar with the whereabouts of one another's banking and investment records. In an emergency, it's a big relief to be able to find things quickly.

• **Compare the results of separate and joint tax returns.**
While most couples can reduce their combined tax liability by
filing jointly, it's best to have an accountant assess your situation
both ways. Filing separately may be preferable to you no matter
what—for ease of accounting or for a fair split of refunds or
payments. You could also file separately just to minimize confusion, but the price of clarity could be high.

~

Farewell, Bachelor Shrine: Your Habitat

For over six years, Apartment 510 was my queendom. It sits in Barbizon Hotel South—a latter-day take on the legendary Manhattan residence for nice young ladies. This Washington condominium is a Twilight Zone dominated by single, mid-life professional women.

"Do not sell to another single woman," my neighbor Amy jokingly threatened.

Apartment 510 was my alter ego. Through the art on the walls and the jumble in the cupboards, she reflected me. From ice storms and office storms, she sheltered me. As I slept, read, daydreamed, or yakked on the phone, she cradled me. Once I married, however, Apartment 510 was an odd place. Whenever I returned, I was unsettled. I didn't belong there. She was the kind of old friend one still cares about even if interacting with her is no longer nourishing. Touching base with her was nice, but I couldn't wait to return *home*, where my marriage resided.

Some mid-life newlyweds have lived together for many years. Your adjustment is nil, unless you deeply contemplate the newness of living together in matrimony. Many of you haven't exactly lived together, but perhaps you've been shifting between two residences for a while. He's had underwear and a few shirts at your place; you've had a full complement of toiletries at his. Each of you still had your own home base. And even if you spend virtually all your time at his place, you're not living together mentally as well as physically until you get rid of your emergency retreat.

A few of us are babes in this wood. Deciding to marry Husband was as easy as a sunny day. Deciding three months earlier to let him move into my apartment was another matter. He'd be wholly in my space! Full-time! Would he like it? Could I stand it? Would he still like me? I was as eager to do this as I was freaked out. Living together would not only feel great; it would confirm whether or not we had the right marital stuff. In the '60's and '70's, many of you laid that argument on your parents. You may have been young and idealistic or young and full of crap. But lo and behold, you were right.

Said Grace to her disapproving mother: "I wouldn't even buy a dress before trying it on first." She's happily wearing the same "dress" some 20 years later.

Couples establishing a mutual nest, before or after marriage, choose her place, his place, or new, neutral territory. The latter is generally recommended, to prevent that awkward host-guest dynamic. You don't want to impose, nor do you want to feel imposed upon. But for mid-life and older couples, economics or emotion may factor more prominently into the decision. Some of us have homes that are just a few years shy of mortgage freedom. Or maybe we've become deeply attached to a neighborhood we've called home for 20 years. Or to the house we fully restored with our own hands.

Elaine owned a large house that she'd recently decorated to the max. Her partner, fresh from a divorce, had a rented apartment and some weight training equipment. When they decided to marry, deciding where to live was a no-brainer.

Shortly after we married, Husband introduced me to his homeland. "I can't wait to show you our house. I hope you like it." I hoped like heck I'd like it, too. Throughout our courtship, he'd talked lovingly of the period house he'd bought and fixed up, only to be relocated overseas when he was done. He talked wistfully of the old fireplace and the kitchen he'd remodeled. If the company ever moved him back to this community, he longed to make this house his home again—and mine.

Suppose I hated it? *No, sweetie, let's ditch this museum and move into that nice new development.* His heart would crumble. But knowing our tastes were compatible, I was optimistic. Fortunately, I found the house and the neighborhood entirely charming. Please let the old bones and organs of the house be as healthy as Husband says.

Now we're building a vacation house in *my* homeland. It's an opportunity to fashion a home from scratch according to *our* vision, even if it's mainly a fulfillment of my longtime dream.

Choosing housing is one thing. Having to choose a city or country is a bigger—and increasingly common—newlywed issue. Many of us fall in love with people in remote places. We have career, family, and emotional ties in one place; our partner has his or hers in another. Will you move so your partner can stay near his children? Will he stay put so you can maintain your catering business? Will he quit his job and move if he's just five years shy of retirement eligibility?

Will you commute? For newlyweds, that's painful. Some couples who've been married a long time actually like the separation. Sometimes they like it so much, they split for good.

Husband and I commuted for an "eternity"—five months—while I eased out of my job. A fellow newlywed at work would speak lovingly of driving to work together in the morning and dining by candlelight at night—every night. Meanwhile, I barely felt married. Moreover, I felt I was missing an arm. The comfortably solo woman was dead.

At long last, I picked up my East Coast roots and transplanted them to Texas, an unfamiliar land of Chevy Suburbans, treeless backyards, and requisite makeup. I fretted that I'd miss Jack Frost nipping at my nose. Instead, without envy I watch northern drivers spin around on the ice on the evening news, then go outside to turn the kabobs on the grill.

"How do you like Texas?" northern friends asked. I didn't really know. Husband is here; I'm a newlywed; I'm happy.

At the whim of Husband's employer, we could wind up just about anywhere else on the planet at any time. I'm game.

All my life, I'd imagined that, if married, I'd still want to have my own room. Not my own *bed*room, but kind of an office/den/playroom/ archives. Like Apartment 510, it would be my private sanctuary. It could house my treasures and tchotchkes that aren't equally favored by Husband. It could be my just-in-case "space," if and when needed. Maybe Husband would appreciate a room of his own, too.

Meantime, we rent a small house that can't accommodate these plans. Yet it kind of makes us feel like a young couple in a cozy starter nest, looking forward to our home of the future. He moved in a year earlier than I, so of course a few changes were in order when The Missus arrived. He helped me fashion an office out of the small den. Otherwise, I largely resisted any urge to reinvent his world. Tempting my hand the most were the kitchen cabinets; they begged for reorganization. I moved the ceramic bowls from head-smashing height on a top shelf and promised myself I'd adjust to everything else.

I ultimately sold 510 to, yes, a single, professional woman. Sorry, Amy. My final bachelor pad was history, leaving me symbolically "stuck" with Husband. I occasionally need space to concentrate on a work project, but so far I haven't needed space on general principle.

To a woman who has lived her whole adulthood in apartments, even a rented house feels like a promotion: Air on all sides. A garden to tend (poorly). Birds to spy at the feeder. A garage! I feel like June Cleaver and, I confess, I like it. In a longtime fantasy, I'm Claire Huxtable, living in an old Brooklyn brownstone—a house with character. But now that I've settled down another notch, the suburbs ain't bad. And for at least as long as newlywed fever persists, this nondescript box will suit me fine.

On Habitat . . .
Consider This

• **Find neutral ground.** If you're living together for the first time, settling in mutually new territory is ideal. But if there's a compelling reason—practical or emotional—for him to move into your existing space, or vice versa, that's fine. One of you may have to make a compromise, but each of you should fully agree to the habitat decision without pressure.

• **Don't be a tree hugger.** Don't cling to an old residence or old community simply for fear of the unknown. Be adventurous.

• **Get rid of the old place.** Don't keep your bachelor shrine for sentimental reasons—or "just in case." That's the wrong newlywed attitude. If it's unwise at the moment for you to sell—due to market conditions, for example, or a dirt-cheap interest rate—consider renting the place out instead.

• **Avoid the commuter marriage.** It's especially tough on newlyweds. It may work temporarily if it begins with a clear end in sight—six months, a year. But avoid commuting as a long-term strategy. It's hazardous to your marital health.

• **Carefully mark your territory.** If you're moving into his space, you've got a juggling act to perform. Do what you can to put your signature on the place and make it feel partially yours. But don't rearrange his world entirely. Likewise, if you're the receiving party, give him some freedom of expression.

• **Create space.** Need your own sense of space within the communal place? Stake out a room to call your own if you can. If your new home is small, at least stake out a corner. At the very least, claim a bookshelf.

~

Pennies from Heck: More Stuff

S ome years back, a friend moved into the apartment of her boyfriend (now husband). On the wall over their bed, he wanted to keep a prized tapestry he'd purchased in his travels. Its subject was a big animal making dinner of a smaller one. My friend didn't find this scene inspiring for sweet dreams, romance or even a passing glance. Compromise: It still hangs in their home, but not in the bedroom.

For mid-life newlyweds who are newly cohabitating, the issue of merging stuff—your stuff, his stuff and yours together—generally pertains to volume more than taste. You realized this when you registered for wedding gifts, if not before. Two complete households are coming together: two master bedrooms, two dining room suites and so on. And most of it's worth keeping. Decent furnishings long ago replaced the sofa from the second-hand store and the kitchen table you found at curbside for your first apartment.

Then there are books, music, art and other collections—maybe 20 years' worth, multiplied by two. At least one partner's "collectibles" may include outright junk—boxes of eight-track tapes, decades of canceled checks or Thigh Masters long forgotten. Think about your parents' attic; you're halfway there.

My most challenging junk was a five-gallon water bottle full of pennies—a few hundred dollars' worth. I started feeding this bottle in my twenties when some friend I thought wise foretold an enormous, long-term hike in the price of copper. Although this wise person never explained to me how to melt pennies down and sell them, I never kicked the habit. A quarter-century later, this bottle is hardly an appropriate furnishing for a grownup, married or single. But it was so heavy and immovable by the time I vacated Apartment 510, I couldn't convince Goodwill Industries to come get it.

Given two full households, something's got to go. You and your partner probably have compatible tastes. Thus, you can readily forgo your china for his. He can give up his towels for yours. Like the animal tapestry, there's sure to be an exception or two to this rule. If you dread the prospect of dining every day on his beloved French rococo table with the roaring-lion feet, you've got to be honest.

You or your partner may also have some of the spoils of divorce or widowhood. One of Husband's remainders was a bed. Their bed. It was retired.

Husband "helped" me move out of 510. "Why are you keeping this?" he asked about this, that, the other, and then some. Despite all I'd already discarded, several remaining items were indeed outdated, worn or useless. Out they went. Other items were still important to me. To heck with Husband; I kept them. I still kind of liked my old metal cart from the Salvation Army with the painted enamel trays. Husband hated it intensely; I let him chuck it. Was this the same guy who was fascinated with my apartment decor at first sight?

Don't obsess if his keepers aren't perfectly symbiotic with yours. Eclectic design can come off beautifully. Try those sleek Italian chairs on the Chinese rug.

No matter how much you've collectively got, you and your partner will go out and get more. Feathering a nest seems to call for shopping. After all, you'll "need" to fill in some of the blanks in your wedding registry. Plus you can't use the tartan plaid towels in the new pastel bathroom. And those cushions you saw on sale would be so comfy on the window seat.

Mid-life men enjoy selecting home furnishings. They've developed definite tastes, and they're not ashamed to be seen in a linen department or a kitchen supply store. Whether or not you can shop well together depends on your respective shopping personalities. Husband had a small tantrum at a garden store one day when I couldn't settle on a color of impatiens. I may be adapting well to partnership, but when it comes to shopping, I'm better off alone. Meantime, I made a rule: *Don't ever get angry with me in front of people again.*

Antiquing is another matter. Husband and I both love old things with character. (I *don't* mean ourselves.) Our idea of a good weekend is to forage together through estate sales, flea markets or antiques shops. A great weekend means finding a miniature cut-crystal perfume bottle or a rare piece in our porcelain pattern—cheap. He's partial to high-brow furnishings at least 100 years old. I lean toward relatively low-brow goods of the early 20th century. As we've grown closer, so have our tastes. I now get as excited as he does over a tarnished old sterling spoon. He's enamored of my '20's vanity, and Art Deco pottery has begun to turn his head.

Looking at the furnishings around our home today, a stranger would guess we're a long-established couple rather than newlyweds. We're all of the above.

From 510, I drove to Goodwill Industries with several cardboard boxes of pennies in my trunk. "If you can get them here, we'll take them," I'd been told. I wondered—on the freeway—how strong my rear axle was. A strong young man unloaded the boxes. Pennies leaked from the seams. I sped off before any boxes collapsed altogether.

When I became a woman, I gave up childish things.

On More Stuff . . .
Consider This

• **Figure out whose bedroom suite becomes *the* bedroom suite.** Same goes for all other duplicates. Give-and-take is key. Keep a vase you love that he doesn't. Then let him keep the weights he never uses. Don't hesitate to compliment him on any belongings you like a lot.

• **Agree on the big things.** It's easy to ignore an ugly bud vase. It's impossible to ignore the living room sofa or the dining room set. If you can't agree on whose to use, start with something entirely different, if possible.

• **Make sure you're represented.** Ultimately, your furnishings—new or old—should reflect both of you. It's okay if one person's original belongings dominate. But each of you should find ample representation of your personal style in the home.

• **Get rid of any lingering junk of your youth.** It's okay to keep a memento or two. Make it a *small* memento, not the penny jar.

• **Be generous with your better cast-offs.** Consider siblings or offspring who can use some decent furnishings. Finally, don't forget charity.

Put on a Sweater, Dear: Meddling

I stare at his naked head as he backs out of the driveway in the convertible. He gets the message.

"I don't need a cap today. It's overcast."

Still, it's July in Texas. After a mere walk across the office parking lot, he'll have a fresh crop of red speckles on his head. That's darn worse than hat-head, and the sun is hazardous to his health to boot. He grumbles and puts his cap on. This time.

His turn: "Have you made an appointment with the doctor about your ear?" he asks. Again.

No, I'm still using the natural ear drops I got at the health food store. Yet another debate ensues about traditional versus nontraditional healing. To him, no medical advice is worthy unless it's cited in the *New England Journal of Medicine*—or unless a supermarket tabloid reports that broccoli kills.

This is *Living Mutually* gone too far. It should be enough that you and your husband have to reach consensus on what to have for dinner, where to go on vacation and the like. On top of that, you'll try to get your partner to do things your way even when the matter has nothing to do with you and everything to do with him. You'll find something you can't help saying about his eating, driving, family relations, office politics or the tie and shirt he's just put on. He'll do the same to you. It's born of caring, but it can become irritating to the beneficiary nonetheless.

"I don't know how I managed to survive all those years before I met you," Husband sometimes wonders sarcastically.

Family relations are a guaranteed hot spot. For several months, Jessica tried to help her new husband heal relations with his daughter, a young woman who was still openly bitter about her parents' divorce. Jessica's suggestions fell on deaf ears every time. She sealed her lips on the subject for good. You've got to know when to quit.

The longer you've run your own life without uninvited "help," the more annoying it is. You'll resist all the more because you're a willful woman. He'll resist all the more because he's The Man. And the longer you've both lived, the less likely it is that either of you is fixable in the first place.

The crux of the problem seems to be that spouses, regardless of age, can't resist the fathering or mothering thing. I catch myself treating Husband like the child I never had. I catch him treating me like the children he *did* have.

"Let me help you with that," he said in the kitchen one day as I prepared to use a knife. "You might cut yourself."

I try to be patient. After all, it was I who ran after him one chilly morning—apron strings flapping!—to give him a sweater. The only thing missing from this picture was a yellow school bus.

In matters of health, diet, and fitness, mid-lifers may be especially meddling. Sickness looms larger for us. Our parents are becoming more bent, more arthritic, maybe even downright ill. Our buddies and coworkers are undergoing back surgery and hysterectomies. They're getting cancer and heart disease. Some die. Of course, *you're* not becoming old and at risk. In the mirror, on a good day, you're still that young chick. You wear jeans; that proves it. You don't need nagging about diet and doctors from your husband; you just need to dish it out.

"I do everything you tell me, dear," he often mocks. Translation:

That's a good idea; I'll do it. I don't hesitate to make suggestions, knowing that he won't hesitate to dig in his heels if he's opposed. However, I can do without the follow-up lesson in quantum physics, explaining why my suggestion is a breach of science.

"I don't have to wait for a rolling boil. See the steam rising off the water? That means the water is 212 degrees Fahrenheit. A rolling boil isn't any hotter than that. . . ."

I finally drew up a code of conduct for myself. One: Express my point of view one time, clearly. Two: Be confident that I've been heard even if it looks like I'm being ignored. Three: Back off. I haven't perfected Three yet. And sometimes I find a novel way to repeat One—like raising an eyebrow instead of commenting aloud when his hand is in the peanut jar.

I should review the code more often. And so should he.

"Don't you know what time it is?" Yes, it's 1:30 in the morning. "Come to bed!"

On Meddling . . .
Consider This

• **Take as well as you give.** It's okay to offer suggestions to one another. You know and love one another well. Try to keep the practice mutual.

• **Don't cross the line into nagging.** It's all in tone and repetition. If you do nag, hear yourself. You'll recognize it when you get that certain look or comment in return. You won't like the way you sound, and that may speed the cure.

• **Don't treat him like a child.** Absolutely avoid giving instructions that your partner outgrew in kindergarten. *There's a car coming; be careful.* Transfer any latent mothering instincts. Volunteer at a day-care center. Get a dog or cat. Even the cat will have her limits.

• **Stay calm.** What if, absent your intervention, your husband seems about to fall off a cliff? What if he's about to blow his relationship with his brother for good? What if he's about to say something at work that may shorten his career? It's still your right to comment. And it's still not your right to nag. You'll be stressed, but remind yourself: He's come pretty far in life in one piece.

~

Dirty Little Hot Dogs: Warts, Wounds, and Other Private Parts

M aybe you wear pantyhose with a secret six-inch run up the thigh. Maybe you faithfully watch some sleazy television tabloid show. Maybe you lick the bottom of the ice cream bowl. For decades, no one has been wise to you but the dog.

Now we share the sanctuary of home full-time with another, and our privacy is just about shot.

Many of our foibles, and his, were evident long before marriage. He already knows the interior of your car is an all-in-one office, snack bar, closet, and storage room. He knows your freezer is a tomb of the unknown. He laughs or looks the other way. Bottom line, he loves you anyway.

Yet no matter how much dirty laundry you've exposed, literally and otherwise, there's bound to be another postnuptial revelation or two. *Uh-oh. Now he's going to find out about* _____.

Privacy may be the reason some of us stayed single so long. It allows us to put our best foot forward while keeping that back foot with the bunions and scuffed-up shoe out of sight.

So much for the bunions and idiosyncrasies you *know* about. In your husband's reflection, you'll discover more.

"You are the most piddling woman," Husband observes. "You can't relax for more than ten minutes." Wow, that's pretty true. On a Saturday, he can busy himself all morning, then sit firmly in one spot and read all afternoon. I generally keep moving—hanging laundry, shuffling papers, transferring things from Point A to Point B. For all my scurrying, I accomplish very little besides avoiding the sin of sloth.

We have three basic alternatives for handling our secret flaws and weird behavior within the context of marriage.

First and best: Reveal your private ways and be free. So what if our partner can't see the wisdom of *Geraldo*? Watch it, and be happy. Let him go somewhere and ponder *Beowulf*.

Two: Keep a few minor habits in the closet. When I was small, my mother loved the hot dogs sold from those colorful, steaming carts on the streets of New York. My father was convinced "those dirty little hot dogs" harbored the next plague. What did Mom do? She took me to the hot dog cart while Dad was at work.

Three: Change. If a habit is truly more faulty than cute in our mind's eye, we can make a newlywed resolution to kick it. Promise yourself: *I'll stop leaving my shoes scattered throughout the house.* As with New Year's resolutions, don't commit to too much. You're pretty well grounded in your ways.

"I have a confession," said Husband many months into our marriage. "Before we got married, I almost never made the bed during the week."

Neither did I. Now here we were, each aiming to live up to the other's standard—a standard that didn't exist. Gradually, bed-making is becoming an actual habit for us, even when it happens just a few hours before bedtime.

Some private matters simply can't be swept under the rug. Two words, mid-lifers: night sweats.

An unmade bed pales in comparison to deeper confidences like childhood bed-wetting, the pain of miscarriage, estrangement from your father. Or perhaps you had a "past," as people used to say. Given your age, maybe you had a *long* past. A friend who married many years ago has never summoned the courage to tell her husband about the abortion she had long before they met. A coworker once computer-dated a woman from across country. She was single with no children, she said in her E-mail to him. Once they were engaged, he learned she was not quite divorced and had children—six of them.

Let's go one deeper: Perhaps you've got some serious current issues, such as alcoholism or clinical depression. If you knew your husband for a considerable time before marriage, he's probably aware. Either you told him, or he figured it out, and in marriage you're handling it hand in hand. If, on the other hand, you're one of those midlifers who marry in a hurry, maybe a critical detail about yourself remains hidden. It won't stay hidden long.

Well into my forties, I felt I could marry only a man with whom I could share absolutely anything. I figured that requirement was so idealistic, I probably could never marry. No man likely existed who could inspire me to open all the doors. I was wrong. Gladly wrong.

In all likelihood, you married a man you trust. Still, it may take time for the private you to exercise that trust and share yourself fully, warts and all. Keeping secrets from the man you love and respect is stressful. How stressful it is depends on whether your secret is hot dogs or substance abuse. It will fester in the back of your brain. It may require you to look over your shoulder for the rest of your life. And sooner or later, it may unravel.

A lot more living is ahead, and more personal wounds are waiting to happen. Some of us long-time singles turn inward when we feel bad. Menstrual cramps or getting downsized may send us into a dark corner like an injured animal. Our husbands may want to help lick our wounds. We may feel awkward about divulging our wounds, let alone having him get involved. We're bashful about exposing them. Besides, we feel no one can do anything about them better than we can. We feel guilty about burdening the man we love. But let's not forget: *For better and for worse . . . in sickness and in health. . . .*

It often works.

On Warts . . .
Consider This

• **Don't agonize about the impending loss of privacy.** Jump into the pool of wedlock, and let the chips fall where they may.

• **Bring issues out of the closet.** If there were big issues in your past, you'll feel better for getting them out in the open—and confirming his unconditional love. If there's a big issue in your present, divulge it for sure. Do it now. Sharing even the worst can strengthen a relationship. Protracted insincerity, on the other hand, will bring it down. It may help to rehearse openness by divulging a "little" secret first.

• **Attempt to correct a personal flaw or two.** Make sure it's a real flaw in your eyes, not just his. Yes, you're an "old dog." Try to learn a new trick anyway.

• **Discover yourself.** Just when you thought you knew yourself, you'll learn more through his eyes. Welcome this continued insight, whether the revelations make you laugh or cringe.

• **Consider a diary.** If you still need a private repository of expression, communicating with a diary is healthier than shedding nothing at all.

Into the Sunset

"How's married life?"
Great.
"Sorry you didn't do it long time ago, huh?"

No. In its time, and for all its time, bachelor life was a treasure—chock full of career, hobbies, friends and adventures. It wasn't a laugh a minute: I endured bad jobs, ridiculous love interests, precarious financial outlooks, an attempted car theft and a bicycle crash that robbed both front crowns. On balance, I had a rich and rewarding time. A strong, consistent bond in love would have been gravy but not the potatoes.

Nonetheless, by my 40th birthday, I sensed that some people looked at me askance. Unlike divorcées, lifelong bachelors must be hard to accept on face value. Sometimes I wanted to release a statement: *I am not psychotic. I am not married to my job. I am not a Lesbian. I am not the world's most impossible bitch to get along with. Though I live in Washington, I am not involved in a highly discreet affair with a prominent news maker. I am simply single.*

Most mid-lifers, single and otherwise, accept themselves calmly and with self-esteem intact. We realize quiet spells at home often trump aimless running around in the streets. We've reconciled with those bubbles of cellulite. We've given up our very wildest dreams and zeroed in on a few realistic ones. We've relaxed.

If we're single, we've also stopped pondering how long the "slow period" is going to last in our love lives. But looking ahead, some of us realize that solo is not the way to grow old. Sooner or later, we know we'll need someone to nourish and be nourished by. And like job hopping, partner hopping in mid-life is pitiful. We need to settle in with someone for the long haul.

Somewhere along the line, societal expectations got out of synch with nature. Age twenty-five or so is probably an excellent starting point for motherhood. Women that age are generally energetic enough and wise enough to do it well. Marriage is another story. Mothers don't necessarily have to know themselves; partners do. Not many women or men do marriage really well before age 30. A few of us slow developers need to wait a good ten years beyond that.

Waiting has at least one down side.

After one of our slow, Sunday breakfasts, I asked Husband if he wanted to go to the health club early or late in the day.

"Maybe later." Pause. "I think I may go to the emergency room in a little while."

What?

Husband had been having consistent heart palpitations. *For four days.* And some pressure near his heart. And a needle-like pain. So he was thinking about going to the hospital, though it seemed a silly thing to do.

What??

The emergency room people promptly plopped him into a wheelchair and rushed him into examination ahead of a waiting room full of people. They wired him every which way to a beeping machine and took some routine blood tests—*the same process my favorite television cop underwent, which revealed an infection that had damaged his heart, so he had to have a transplant, but they couldn't find a donor, and when they did, the new heart didn't take well, so . . .*

They kept Husband overnight for observation and a stress test the next day. I slept alone at home in an immense and empty bed.

Death parted Aunt Bern and her husband within five years of their wedding. Though Bern was in resounding despair when Elgy died, I figured, Bern can come through this. Unlike widows who'd been married since their teens, Bern knew how to live independently. She'd been accustomed to bachelorhood most of her life; she could get accustomed to it again. I don't think she ever totally did.

"I'm on my way home," Husband reported perkily in the morning. "The doctor says I have the healthiest heart they've ever tested."

I hadn't realized the weight of the mighty sandbags I bore those 24 hours until they took wing. Nor had I acknowledged the nightmare I'd glimpsed of a future without Husband. It was odd and unfathomable. Like Bern, I'd been a wholly functional bachelor darn near forever. But I didn't know that bachelor any more. She was a stranger to me.

At best, mid-life couples can look forward to half a lifetime of togetherness. We don't dwell on that fact, however. Most times, we feel like any other wild and crazy kids, happily starting our journey into the ever after. We dream the dreams of mid-lifers: retirement, travels, grandchildren. We dream those dreams as if we have infinite time to work them all in. Only once in a while it occurs to us that we don't. Even then, we're in no way discouraged.

Everything our married friends, acquaintances, mothers, television sitcoms and women's magazines say about marriage turns out to be true. You know the adages: You've got to work at it constantly. You've got to take the bitter with the sweet. It's like baking bread: You never know how it's going to come out, but the reward is in the mixing, kneading and molding.

More discoveries: Husbands lift 40-pound bags of potting soil! They shovel snow! They can slay the mighty Texas roach! It's refreshing to have manly support on an everyday basis. In no time, we evolve from wrestling for the right to carry our own suitcase to saying: "Sweetie, would you get that?" This marital fringe benefit is all the sweeter for our mid-life knowledge, born of long experience, that we're capable of hauling the suitcase on our own.

On the flip side, we don't wear the old gender roles of our mothers singlehandedly, and we marry men who don't expect us to. Husband cooks and launders and such without the slightest prodding. The nut actually enjoys polishing silver. Yet at the end of the day, if there's neither a pot on the stove or a plan in my head, I often hear Betty Crocker whispering "tsk, tsk."

But Betty, I've been working all day, just like he has.

Yes, but you've been working at home. *You could have done* something. . . .

I continue to strive to shut this woman up. Yet I don't mind taking pride in a recipe that makes my husband say "aaaahh," the selection of just the right placemats for the dinette or the glory of every new blossom on my African daisy. I enjoy my occasional successes in life. If some are "feminine" successes, so what? And I'm fully settled into my new private-life name, though I'm less than comfortable hearing "Mrs." in front of it. It makes me feel like an appendage.

Marriage is one part unconditioned response. Even for the novice, it's as amazingly natural as breathing. The other part is conscious and specific learning.

If I say I'm not crazy about Shirt A with Tie B, what are the odds that Husband will protest? (100%) What are the odds that he will change the tie? (75%)

We never graduate; the school of marriage is forever. Yet with varying rates of speed and agility, we can grow and excel in this school at any age. We learn when to speak up and when to bite our tongues. We learn when to ask, when to consult, and when to act empowered. We learn what's better done mutually or separately. We jointly figure out the quandaries of money and material things. We learn how to comfort and be comforted. We learn to read eyes, body language and tone of voice. We discover facets of ourselves we'd never seen. We learn trust works. And when we need space, we figure out how and where to find it.

That's the strangest revelation of all: I rarely need space. Husband and I call each other once or twice a day from our desks for no good reason. On weekends, we do most things together, from Kmart to the movies. We rarely jump in separate cars to do our separate things. Together, we take up about a third of the must-have king-sized bed. If we're apart for a day or two, we hate it. I thought I'd relish the chance to do "my thing," only to find I barely remember what it is. Some aspects of my thing have become *our* thing, which I no longer enjoy doing alone so much.

Friend Jeanne knows what I mean. As her husband's unofficial traveling secretary, she's with him on the job and off. "What surprises me most is that we're together literally every day—day and night—and we still can't get enough of each other."

Maybe this means all our decades of space were sufficient. Then again, when newlywed fever wears off, will we wake up screaming one morning, jump in our cars and take off on sabbatical?

Sooner or later, significant others adapt to our marriages also. Immediately after the wedding, as I finished packing—okay—the *trousseau*, I noticed the cat eyeballing me with tremendous expression.

It's all over for us now, isn't it?

No, I assured him, it wasn't. But little did he know he was on the verge of making serious adjustments of geography, habitat and—in the utmost indignity—household rank. He made it easy on himself by believing that he now owned two people instead of one. He may have been right.

Just like our pets, most of our guarded in-laws, wary step-people, disgruntled children, nervous friends or skeptical bosses sooner or later make peace with our marriages and relax. They see *we're* at peace and relaxed. We didn't smell the coffee and get an annulment a week later. So they figure they might as well relax, too. If we're really fortunate, they're also happy for us. We'll settle for relaxed.

I get tremendous joy out of being Dad's wife. Appropriately, I'm not the "other mother" to these men, except when there's more than a dozen empty soda cans around the living room. But once in a while, I'm summoned for expert advice on making French toast or getting wrinkles out of graduation gowns. I wing it. And frying up a whole pound of bacon and a carton of eggs for a bunch of ravenous guys is fun every now and then if you haven't been doing it every morning for your entire adult life.

Mom looks forward to visits from the son-in-law with the tools. Even in his healthiest, most energetic days, my father was not what you'd call handy. Light bulb out? Call the electrician. Husband, on the other hand, can fix a host of household ills, from rusty retractable garbage cans to rusty daughters. I believe Mom is also comforted knowing I won't grow old alone.

"You're the best wife!" Husband occasionally exclaims. I'm the tougher judge; I give myself a B-minus. I give myself an A-plus, however, for marrying whom I did when I did. It's my life's crowning achievement. I've never exercised better judgment. And my timing was every bit as critical as my choice of Husband.

Our marriage thus far is a lot like our wedding—imperfectly glorious. Good partnership beats good solitude. It *is* the potatoes, not the gravy, in life. I learn that anew every day.